AF702464

The Interpreter's Quick Guide to Self-Employment

2nd Edition

By

Rosemary Johnson and Brent Bocian

LABYRINTH
PUBLISHING GROUP

Copyright © 2019
by Labyrinth Publishing Group

All rights reserved. No part of this publication may be reproduced, distributed, or transmitted in any form or by any means, including photocopying, recording, or other electronic or mechanical methods, without the prior written permission of the publisher, except in the case of brief quotations embodied in critical reviews and certain other noncommercial uses permitted by copyright law.

For permission requests, desk copy requests and general questions, please email Rosemary@QuickGuideTax.com

Printed in the United States of America
Labyrinth Publishing Group
Washington, DC

ISBN: 9781097365234

Quick Guide Tax

Tax Services Designed For Freelance ASL Interpreters

Professional Tax Services

Work with the authors to file your taxes!
Get resources & support throughout the year, guided application of the concepts in this book and a stress-free tax filing experience.

Financial Coaching

Work with the authors to learn financial strategies including debt management, budgeting, insurance, retirement, estate planning and more.

Workshops

Any content from this book can be used to create a custom workshop for your local interpreting community.

Interested? Visit our website at
www.QuickGuideTax.com

@QuickGuideTax

Follow us for business, tax & finance tips!

Disclaimer

The information contained within this book is provided for informational purposes only. Neither Ms. Johnson nor Mr. Bocian are lawyers, and the information in this book should not be considered legal advice. You should always seek appropriate counsel for your own situation. Readers are advised not to act upon this information without seeking the service of a tax professional.

Accuracy of Information

While the authors have endeavored to furnish accurate and up-to-date information, they do not warrant that any information contained in, or made available through, this book is accurate, complete, reliable, current or error free. We assume no liability or responsibility for any errors or omissions in this book.

Disclaimer of Warranties and Limitations of Liability

Use of this book is at your own risk. We disclaim all warranties; neither our suppliers nor we shall be held liable for any damages of any kind, which may be incurred through the use of this book.

Links to Third Party Websites

For your convenience, this book may contain hyperlinks to websites and servers maintained by third parties. We do not control, evaluate, endorse or guarantee the content found in those sites. We do not assume any responsibility or liability for the actions, products, services and content of these sites or the parties that operate them. Your use of such sites is at your own risk.

Table of Contents

PREFACE

The interpreting profession varies greatly based on the languages you provide services for and the overall need for interpreters in those languages. Because the profession is so diverse, interpreters often approach their work differently from one another. Interpreters come in all shapes and sizes, and what works for one may not work for another. For this reason, some may choose to be a salaried employee, some to be a self-employed freelancer, and some may switch between both at different points in their career. This book is written for those who choose the self-employed 'freelance' route.

The common accounting term used for someone who provides services, but is not an employee of a company, is an independent contractor or "IC". In the interpreting field, the term 'freelancer' is often used interchangeably with IC. An IC is typically paid a flat rate (either hourly, by project, etc.) and is subject to a service contract or agreement that includes terms negotiated by themselves and the business entity they are providing interpreting services for.

In the following chapters we will touch briefly on topics such as taxes, business structure, deductions, bookkeeping, self-care, retirement, and much more. Our goal is to give interpreters insight into how to run their freelance endeavors like a well-organized small business. For example: Are you taking advantage of every possible tax deduction? Are you familiar with retirement options? Are you familiar with bookkeeping? Do you know the difference between being a sole proprietor versus having an LLC?

We will answer these common questions in an effort to introduce you to what the world of freelance business is all about. During the creation of this book we combined our personal and professional experiences with advice from several CPAs, tax preparers, seasoned interpreters, tax attorneys, financial planners and business consultants to help verify the topics covered in the following pages. We hope this information provides you with the inspiration to research more about your own unique situation and be proactive in talking to a professional on ways that you can operate your business more efficiently and profitably.

CHAPTER 1: TAXES

The topic of taxes for the interpreting field is an on-going discussion with countless concerns including which tax deductions are allowed: travel expenses, home office, meals, etc. We often hear fears of owing the IRS thousands of dollars at the end of the year and not being prepared for the financial strain. The most frustrating part of this quandary is that there is no single correct answer. It seems that different interpreters are given vastly different - and often conflicting - information about taxes, which contributes to the massive confusion. It's time for us, as members of our professional field, to become more knowledgeable about why we are paying so much in taxes and how we can take control of our finances.

Being a freelance interpreter is essentially owning a small business. Consequently, we can learn a great deal by analyzing how other small businesses are run, both financially and operationally. Taxes can be one of the biggest expenses for businesses. Therefore, we must become more educated about how the tax system functions in order to understand why we might owe taxes one year, and yet get money back as a tax refund another year. Wrapping your head around this system will provide you with a better understanding of how to control your cash flow and expenses. Not knowing how the tax system works might cause you to owe much more than you should at the end of the year.

In a nutshell, there are three types of taxes that are most commonly paid on the income you earn annually; (1) Social Security & Medicare taxes (also known as self-employment taxes or FICA taxes), (2) federal income taxes and (3) state/local income taxes. According to the IRS's website (www.IRS.gov) – Social Security tax is charged at 12.4% and Medicare at 2.9%, for a combined total of 15.3%. Federal income tax follows a bracket system to determine the amount you will have to pay annually. State and local income tax rates vary and can be found through a simple online search.

Types of Tax	How Much we Pay
Social Security & Medicare tax *Known as "FICA" for employees, or "Self-employment Tax" for freelancers*	15.3% (Social Security: 12.4%, Medicare: 2.9%)
Federal Income Tax	Percent based on brackets
State & Local Income Tax	Percent varies by state

Different Types of Taxes we Pay

Independent Contractor vs. Employee

Before diving deeper into taxes, let's begin by exploring the difference between an independent contractor versus an employee. In simple terms, if you filled out a W-4 form prior to working with a company, you will receive a W-2 at the end of the year and are typically considered an employee. The form W-2 states your wages for the year along with the taxes that have already been deducted from your wages. If you filled out a W-9 form prior to working with a company, you will receive a 1099-MISC at the end of the year and are considered an independent contractor/self-employed. The form 1099-MISC states the amount paid to you for the year through that company and usually no taxes have been deducted from the amount.

Now, let's look at the differences between these two statuses as it relates to taxes. As previously mentioned, FICA tax is comprised of Social Security and Medicare and totals 15.3%. These same taxes are also called self-employment taxes or payroll taxes. FICA is called self-employment tax for those who are self-employed. FICA is also sometimes called payroll tax for companies with employees. So, if you are an employee you pay FICA, and if you are an independent contractor you pay self-employment tax.

If you are a W-2 employee, your employer pays half of these FICA taxes for you; so only 6.2% of your earnings will be deducted to pay towards Social Security and 1.45% towards Medicare. Whereas freelancers are responsible for paying ALL of their self-employment taxes. This comes out to a grand total of 15.3% (12.4% + 2.9%). However, the good news is that half of this self-employment tax is deductible on your individual tax return. So, although you pay the entire 15.3% initially, the IRS allows you to subtract half of it at the end of the year.

Self-employed (1099)	Salaried employee (W-2)
You are responsible for paying all of your self-employment taxes (15.3%) initially. You deduct half of this amount on your individual taxes.	You pay half of your FICA taxes (7.65%). These are deducted from your paycheck before you receive it. Your employer pays the remaining half (7.65%)

Social Security and Medicare Taxes:
Self-employed vs Salaried Employee

Remember, self-employment tax is owed in addition to your federal and state/local income taxes (see income tax brackets figure). How federal and state taxes are paid also differs between employees and independent contractors. If you are an employee, the employer deducts a certain amount from your paycheck and pays federal and state taxes on your behalf. The amount deducted and paid on your behalf is determined by how you fill out your W-4 form prior to working with the company. If you are an independent contractor, you are responsible for paying your federal and state income taxes yourself through estimated quarterly payments (more on this later in the chapter). Keep in mind that both employees and independent contractors are responsible for paying all of their federal and state income taxes. The difference is that employees make the payments through their employer, and independent contractors make the payments themselves. The sum of all these taxes (self-employment tax + federal income taxes + state/local income taxes) can result in freelancers owing a significant amount at the end of the year if they don't prepare accordingly.

Tax rate	Single filers	Married filing jointly or qualifying widow(er)	Head of household	Married filing separately
10%	\$0-\$9,700	\$0-\$19,400	\$0-\$13,850	\$0-\$9,700
12%	\$9,700-\$39,475	\$19,400-\$78,950	\$13,850-\$52,850	\$9,700-\$39,475
22%	\$39,475-\$84,200	\$78,950-\$168,400	\$52,850-\$84,200	\$39,475-\$84,200
24%	\$84,200-\$160,725	\$168,400-\$321,450	\$84,200-\$160,700	\$84,200-\$160,725
32%	\$160,725-\$204,100	\$321,450-\$408,200	\$160,700-\$204,100	\$160,725-\$204,100
35%	\$204,100-\$510,300	\$408,200-\$612,350	\$204,100-\$510,300	\$204,100-\$306,175
37%	Over \$510,300	Over \$612,350	Over \$510,300	Over \$306,175

2019 IRS Federal Tax Brackets

How Tax Brackets Work

In 2017, the new Tax Cuts and Jobs Act (TCJA) was passed. With this law there have been significant changes to the IRS Tax Bracket and how American citizens are taxed. To better illustrate how tax brackets work, we will quote a revised excerpt from www.TaxACT.com:

Say you're single with no dependents, and your taxable income is $9,000. Your marginal tax rate, according to the 2019 Federal Income Tax Brackets chart, is 10%. You pay $900 in income tax. That's simple.

What if your taxable income is $19,000?

As a Single filer, you're now in the 12% tax bracket. That doesn't mean you pay 12% on all your income, however.

You pay 10% on the first $9,700 plus 12% of the amount over $9,700.

Here's the math:

1st tax bracket: $9,700 X 10% =	$970.00
2nd tax bracket: ($19,000 – $9,700) X 12% =	$1,116.00
Total income tax:	$2,086.00

<u>What if your taxable income is $115,000?</u>

As a Single filer, you've now moved up to the 24% tax bracket, so things get a bit more complicated. In this case:

You pay 10% on the first $9,700,
plus 12% of the amount between $9,700 and $39,475,
plus 22% of the amount between $39,475 and $84,200,
plus 24% of the amount over $84,200.

Here's the math:

1st tax bracket: $9,700 X 10% =	$970.00
2nd tax bracket: ($39,475 – $9,700) X 12% =	$3,573.00
3rd tax bracket: ($84,200 – $39,475) X 22% =	$9,839.50
4th tax bracket: ($115,000 – $84,200) X 24% =	$7,392.00
Total income tax:	$21,774.50

According to the Tax Cuts and Jobs Act, pass-through businesses taxed at the top tax brackets (32% and above), may qualify to have 30% of their net income taxed at the 25% rate. Since the majority of self-employed interpreters do not earn enough to put them in these top tax brackets, this new 25% maximum would not apply.

Quarterly Estimated Tax Payments

As mentioned previously, W-2 employees do not have to worry about paying quarterly estimates. As an employee, your taxes are withheld from your wages by your employer and are deducted each time you receive a paycheck. The employer then deposits those withholdings into an IRS approved bank account.

If you are self-employed you need to pay these taxes yourself. Since freelancers are their own boss (hence the title 'self-employed'), they are responsible for withholding taxes for themselves. This is done by paying an estimated amount in taxes every three months (called quarterlies). These estimated taxes include self-employment, federal and state income tax. Many interpreters assume that you do not have to pay quarterlies, yet the IRS states on their website that "taxes must be paid as you earn income."

If you overpay your estimated taxes, you may receive a refund at the end of the year and, conversely, if you underpay your quarterlies you will owe additional money when you file your year-end tax return. If this is your first year freelancing and you have no prior year tax return to refer to, a tax professional can help calculate your quarterlies for you. Generally speaking, checking with a tax professional can be helpful if you are unsure of how much your estimated quarterly taxes should be.

The IRS states that you can choose to pay your estimated taxes online. There is an Electronic Federal Tax Payment System (EFTPS) through which individuals and businesses can make their payments. This system is particularly helpful because it automatically keeps track of your payment history and the dates when payments were submitted.

As of 2019, the due date for each federal quarterly payment is:

- First quarter (Jan 1 - Mar 31) - taxes are due April 15.
- Second quarter (April 1 - May 31) - taxes are due June 17.
- Third quarter (June 1 - Aug 31) - taxes are due Sept 16.
- Fourth quarter (Sept 1 - Dec 31) - taxes are due Jan 15th of the next year for individuals, and on December 15th for corporations.

IMPORTANT REMINDERS

Due dates for state/local quarterlies may differ from the above federal due dates. Be sure to double-check when your state quarterlies are due. If the payment due date falls on a holiday or weekend, the payment will be on-time if it is submitted online or postmarked on the next business day.

Choosing a Tax Professional

Working with a trusted tax professional can be extremely valuable for freelance interpreters. For the purpose of this book, we consider a tax professional to be either a Certified Public Accountant (CPA), an Enrolled Agent (EA), or a professional tax preparer. CPAs must have a degree in accounting as well as pass a four-part comprehensive exam that covers both tax law and accounting concepts. EAs must pass a three-part comprehensive exam that solely focuses on tax law and legal representation; it does not include any accounting concepts. Both of these statuses are recognized by the IRS and are allowed to handle all types of tax situations. Although a professional tax preparer must have knowledge of the tax law and a preparer tax identification number in order to file for clients, they do not have to necessarily pass any exam to achieve this title.

Due to the density of the tax law, most tax professionals have a niche, or area of expertise. For example, if an experienced CPA works mainly with real estate investors, a majority of their knowledge may be on the complexities of how taxes apply to that unique profession. Although this same experienced CPA holds all the necessary credentials to also file an interpreter's taxes, they may not be familiar with the interpreting profession and potentially overlook tax saving opportunities. Just because someone holds a CPA or EA status does not guarantee they are the best fit for your needs.

Often interpreters assume that if someone is an EA or a CPA, that they know all answers when it comes to taxes; this is not always the case. Tax professionals are human and although they may have honest intentions in how they interpret the tax law, in the end it is just that, their *interpretation* of the tax law. As interpreters, we know first-hand how an interpretation varies from one person to another. This is why one tax professional may give you a different answer than another. The best approach is to be curious, ask a lot of questions and be an active participant in your tax planning.

When choosing your tax professional, it's best to schedule an initial meeting to ask about their experience working with independent contractors and single member businesses. Ask them questions about what you read in this book and see if they are familiar with the business structures and deductions discussed. Be willing to interview several tax professionals before making a final decision.

Conclusion

As freelancers it can be tempting to simply interpret, live paycheck to paycheck and pray that we don't owe a lot in taxes at the end of the tax year. Although it takes a little extra effort to get started, there are many benefits to treating your freelance interpreting career as a true small business. By following common small business practices we, as freelancers, can take advantage of being independent contractors by understanding our taxes, actively working with a tax professional and appropriately budgeting for our quarterly estimated taxes. This way we can all breathe a little easier at the end of the year.

CHAPTER MAIN POINTS

- Key Concept: Understanding how freelancers and W-2 employees are taxed.

Types of Tax	How Much we Pay
Social Security & Medicare tax *Known as "FICA" for employees, or "Self-employment Tax" for freelancers*	15.3% (Social Security: 12.4%, Medicare: 2.9%)
Federal Income Tax	Percent based on brackets
State & Local Income Tax	Percent varies by state

	Employee	Independent Contractor
Form you fill out	W-4	W-9
Form you receive	W-2	1099
How taxes are paid	The employer pays on your behalf	You pay estimated taxes quarterly

TAKE ACTION!

1. Download the app "Stride Tax" to track your business income and deductions (see Chapter 3). This app will calculate how much you should pay in quarterlies throughout the year.

2. At the end of the tax year, go to www.irscalculators.com/tax-brackets-calculator to find out how much you will owe in taxes.

   How much I'll owe: ___________

   Once you get this number, subtract how much you already paid in quarterlies.

   __________ - _____________ = __________

   (what I owe) *(quarterlies paid)* *(final number)*

   If this final number is positive, then that's how much taxes you will **owe** the IRS.

   If this final number is negative, then that's how much money you will get **paid back** from the IRS via a tax refund.

CHAPTER 2: BUSINESS STRUCTURES

By using the small business model as a guidepost, one of your main objectives as a freelance interpreter is to produce a profit. If you're spending a majority of your income on taxes, then obviously you will be left with less profit than you want. One of the best ways to operate a single member business (like being a freelance interpreter) is proper tax planning and asset protection. One way to protect your assets is through your business structure. In this chapter we will discuss the basic types of business structures that are most common among freelance interpreters. Please consult a tax professional or attorney for more information regarding these business structures and for help deciding which one works best for your situation. Keep in mind that this book is not intended to explain how to set up your business structure; it is merely an introduction to what options are available.

Sole Proprietorship

The most basic type of business structure is the sole proprietorship. If you woke up this morning and decided to start freelance interpreting without filing any forms or documentation, you are automatically considered a sole proprietor. The Small Business Administration (www.SBA.gov) states that a sole proprietorship "is the simplest and most common structure chosen to start a business. It is an unincorporated business owned and run by one individual with no distinction between the business and the owner."

In other words, there is no legal paperwork to be filled out for the IRS because it is an unincorporated business. Furthermore, the SBA states that as a sole proprietor, there is no distinction between you and the business; you are responsible for all of the business profits, losses, liabilities and debts - including taxes. This is because the income that your 'business' makes is also your personal income. There is no separation between you and your business.

You, the owner, report income and expenses onto what is called a Schedule C, and then these numbers are 'passed though' directly on your personal tax return form 1040. As previously described, you are personally responsible for paying all self-employment taxes, federal income taxes and state income taxes. For further information please seek advice from a qualified tax professional, and/or refer to the Small Business Administration's website at www.sba.gov/starting-business/choose-your-business-structure/sole-proprietorship.

One of the advantages of a sole proprietorship is that it is easy to set up because there are no state filings, no bylaws and no start-up fees. One of the disadvantages is the amount of liability you incur. The SBA states, "... you can be held personally liable for the debts and obligations of the business." If someone sues your sole proprietor business, they are, in essence, suing you personally and if they win, they can pursue your personal assets (your house, car, etc.).

Mark Kohler, a CPA, attorney and author of *The Tax and Legal Playbook*, cautions that even if you don't have a house or equity, in a lawsuit you could get a judgment or a lien levied against you. That kind of lawsuit could result in affecting your credit or a garnishment on your business income. Some sole proprietors purchase Professional Liability Insurance to add coverage in the event of a lawsuit (discussed later), while others opt to change their business structure to a limited liability company, commonly referred to as an LLC.

Limited Liability Company

According to the SBA, a limited liability company (LLC) "is a structure that provides the limited liability features of a corporation." According to Garrett Sutton, attorney and advisor to Robert Kiyosaki's 'Rich Dad' team, an LLC allows you to protect your assets and personal wealth. If you were to be sued for any reason your assets, such as your residence, bank accounts and investments would be protected because they wouldn't be considered the property of your LLC (discussed later). Your LLC conducts business separately from you, therefore separating your business from your personal assets/wealth. This separation and protection is often referred to as a 'corporate veil'.

In order to keep your LLC status, you can't just file the proper LLC legal papers and forget about it; you must maintain the required practices of an LLC to receive the protection the corporate structure offers. Maintaining the corporate veil, or corporate protection, is vital to ensuring you are properly implementing the protection provided by the law. Maintenance of such structural requirements like separate bank accounts, logging annual meeting minutes, keeping corporate records and using the company name on documents, are all essential components of maintaining the corporate veil. Failure to adhere to these practices may result in the 'piercing' of your corporate veil. In other words, if you are sued and it is determined that your company isn't acting like a real company, your personal assets may be in jeopardy.

There are many different scenarios to consider. The purpose of this book is to simply provide readers with a basic understanding of the entity structures. Please consult an attorney for more information.

The Tax Structure of an LLC

Just because you have an LLC that provides you with asset protection, it doesn't necessarily mean you have tax advantages. A single-member LLC is actually considered a "disregarded entity" and is taxed as a sole proprietorship by default. Many interpreters assume that because they form an official business like an LLC, or a partnership, that it will result in tax savings. This is not necessarily the case.

The single-member LLC is a pass-through entity just like a sole proprietorship. This means all of the profits and losses flow to the owner's personal tax return. The single-member LLC does not pay taxes directly to the IRS. Rather, the owner is responsible for paying the LLC's taxes.

Sole Proprietor vs. LLC

To recap, a sole proprietor structure does not provide you with asset protection but the LLC does, as long as the business is operated according to structural requirements. When it comes to paying taxes, both LLC owners and sole proprietors are treated the same. They both pass-through all business profits or losses onto your personal tax return when you calculate your total income. An LLC won't necessarily impact how you pay self-employment taxes unless it is taxed as what is known as an S Corporation, which is described in the next section.

If an interpreter wanted the asset protection of an LLC but did NOT want to be taxed as a sole proprietor, the IRS offers LLCs the option to elect a tax status and be taxed as either an S Corp or a C Corp. This means the LLC can be taxed as a corporation instead of a sole proprietor. This book will only discuss S Corps. Feel free to contact a tax professional or an attorney if you are interested in finding out about electing C Corp status.

LLC S Corporation

This structure is a bit more complicated and may or may not be suitable for your situation. Please seek advice from your attorney or tax professional on whether or not an S Corp is a good fit. Simply put, an LLC S Corp structure allows an individually owned business to have a separate life from the owner (sometimes referred to as the shareholder). The company would continue to do business even if the owner/shareholder left. Even though an LLC taxed as an S Corp is also considered a pass-through entity just like a regular LLC and sole proprietorship, it is different structurally and has very specific tax reporting requirements.

Taxes and the LLC S Corp

By being an LLC S Corp there are certain regulations, which must be followed if you are to be compliant with the law. These regulations include: requiring scheduled director and shareholder meetings, taking minutes during those meetings, adoption of, and updates to, by-laws, stock transfers, payroll, and the maintenance of records. In addition, the SBA states, "all states do not tax S Corps equally." Please consult with your tax professional and attorney before moving forward with establishing an S Corp.

If you make your freelance interpreting business into an LLC S Corp, you play two roles. You are 1) the owner and 2) a formal employee of your own business. That means you hire yourself as a W-2 salaried employee. The IRS allows this double role to occur when you pay yourself a "reasonable compensation" as an employee. With this double role, your business must set up a payroll process through which you pay yourself W-2 wages. Ultimately, your business would be withholding 7.65% FICA taxes from your wages by way of the W-2 compensation and pay the remaining 7.65% from the business bank account. One disadvantage of being an 'employer' to your W-2 self, is that you may be required to pay FUTA (unemployment taxes).

According to the IRS, "your share of S corporation income isn't self-employment income and it isn't subject to self-employment tax." This means that your W-2 salary would be subject to both FICA and income tax, while your owner's distributions, or your share, would only be subject to income tax. The money you pay yourself through an owner's distribution is taxed less. As an LLC S Corp, your company could pay you a portion of earnings as a reasonable salary (paying FICA and federal/state taxes) and then another portion of earnings as a shareholder's distributions (paying ONLY federal/state taxes). On the other hand, as an LLC without an S Corp tax election, you would pay self-employment tax, federal and state tax on ALL earnings.

When choosing your reasonable salary, consider what you would normally be paid when providing interpreting services in a staff position. Single member LLC S Corps should be cautious when determining a reasonable salary. If you take an extremely low salary, the government may penalize you. Ask your tax professional or attorney for help if you are unsure how to determine what salary you should be paid.

Playing Defense with Business Structure

As independent contractors, it's important to consider asset protection. By not preparing in this regard, interpreters put themselves at risk of severe financial strain in the event of a lawsuit. Although many are aware that they need asset protection, there's a lot of confusion around what kind and how much is needed. For the sake of this book, we will talk about two methods of protection: (1) having an LLC and (2) having professional liability insurance.

Professional liability/errors and omissions insurance offers financial coverage for claims or lawsuits against you for breach of contract, oversights, errors or providing substandard/incomplete work. Insurance for your business can assist paying for attorney fees, court costs, settlements or judgements associated with the lawsuit.

As mentioned previously, an LLC provides interpreters with a "corporate veil" protecting their personal assets from being pursued during a lawsuit. Having and LLC can help make sure your personal assets aren't at risk during the lawsuit.

The easiest way to explain the difference between having an LLC versus having professional liability insurance is with a simple analogy (see following figure). Picture yourself standing across from an entity that's suing you. If you have an LLC, picture yourself now holding a shield. If you were to get sued, your corporate veil would not allow the lawsuit to pursue your personal assets. The LLC is protection between you and the entity suing you. If you also have professional liability insurance, picture a large bag of money laying in front of you. This insurance helps cover legal fees, etc. related to the lawsuit. Therefore, with both a shield (LLC) and the bag of money (liability insurance), an interpreter is prepared for a lawsuit.

How much asset protection an interpreter chooses to get greatly depends on their unique situation. However, in our professional opinion, we have ranked types of asset protection from the low risk to high risk. We encourage interpreters to consult with a professional to determine appropriate coverage.

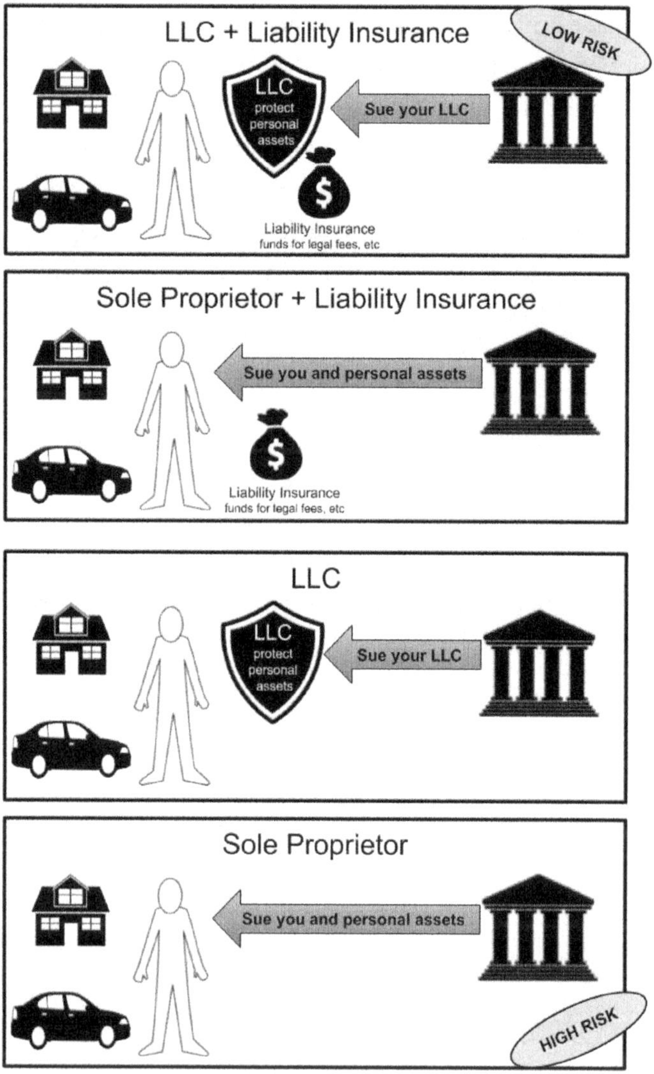

Asset Protection Ranked Safest to Riskiest

Conclusion

If an interpreter starts working and does not opt to establish some alternative form of business structure, they will automatically be classified as a sole proprietor. They will then have to pay self-employment tax and income taxes on ALL of their net income. Becoming an LLC increases asset protection, but you are still taxed as a sole proprietor by default. If you elect to be an LLC S Corp there are more strict tax reporting requirements and owner/shareholders must be paid a reasonable salary. Consider how much asset protection you would like to have through business structure and insurance. Keep in mind that there are coverage limitations and it's recommended to consult with a professional. Many of the concepts discussed in this chapter are discussed in greater depth in Garrett Sutton's book *Start Your Own Corporation*. If an interpreter is ready to select a business or tax classification, they can either consult an accountant, a lawyer or www.legalzoom.com to finalize paperwork.

CHAPTER MAIN POINTS

- Key Concept: Understand different entity structures and asset protection.

Entity	Advantages	Disadvantages
Sole Proprietor	Cheapest and easiest to setup.	No asset protection. Taxed on all earnings (self-employment + income tax).
LLC Tax status: Sole Proprietor	Asset protection.	Must comply with regulations (meetings, records, etc.). Taxed on all earnings (self-employment + income tax).
LLC Tax election: S Corp	Asset protection. Taxed fully on W-2 employee salary (FICA + Income Tax). Only pay income tax on shareholder's distribution.	Must comply with regulations (meetings, records, payroll, etc.). More complicated to maintain, FUTA tax and an extra filing fee.

TAKE ACTION!

1. Take a look at the advantages and disadvantages listed on the previous page. Consider your current situation and choose a business structure and tax classification that's the best fit for you.

□ Sole Proprietorship
□ LLC
□ LLC: S Corp
□ Other ____________________

2. Are you planning on purchasing professional liability insurance?

□ Yes
□ No

3. By choosing this business structure or insurance, what will happen if someone sues you? Refer to the diagrams in the chapter.

□ I will have asset protection AND financial coverage to pay for legal fees, etc.
□ I will ONLY have asset protection
□ I will ONLY have financial coverage to pay for legal fees, etc.
□ I will no asset protection

4. By choosing this business structure, how will you be taxed?

☐ I will be taxed fully on all of my earnings.

☐ My W-2 earnings will be subject to FICA and income tax. My owner's distributions will only be subject to income tax.

5. To begin the process of creating a business/tax structure, speak to a tax professional or visit www.legalzoom.com to get started on paperwork. Which one will you do?

☐ I will speak to a tax professional.

☐ I will visit www.legalzoom.com.

6. If you're interested in professional liability/errors and omissions insurance, search online for three companies you'd like to get a quote from.

1.

2.

3.

CHAPTER 3: DEDUCTIONS

While taxes are likely to be the largest single expense of your business, as well as the most worrisome topic at the end of the year, deductions, on the other hand, are the superheroes to your business. These superheroes go to battle for you throughout the year to save you money. Handling your business tax deductions correctly is just as important as the income you make as an interpreter. In the end, money saved is money earned. Becoming educated on deductions that the IRS allows you to make on behalf of your business can save you from paying high amounts of taxes and put more money back in your pocket.

First, we will provide an overly simplified illustration showing you how deductions work. Let's say you earned $40,000 from freelance interpreting as a sole proprietor (which is what you are if you haven't chosen an entity structure). During that same year let's assume that you had $10,000 in business expenses (maybe you went to an interpreting conference, had some business-related travel expenses and bought a laptop to use solely for interpreting). If that $10,000 is tax deductible, you are allowed to subtract - or deduct - that amount from your $40,000 gross income and pay taxes only on the remaining (net) amount. When your net income is lower, you save on FICA taxes, and you fall into a lower federal tax bracket; resulting in owing less on taxes at the end of the year.

EXAMPLE 1:

1. You earned $40,000 gross income.
2. You spent $10,000 on tax-deductible business expenses.
3. You are only required to pay taxes on $30,000 (net income).

Now let's consider what happens if you had fewer tax-deductible expenses, which are also referred to as write offs.

EXAMPLE 2:

1. You earned $40,000 gross income.
2. You spent $4,000 on tax-deductible business expenses.
3. You pay taxes on $36,000 (net income).

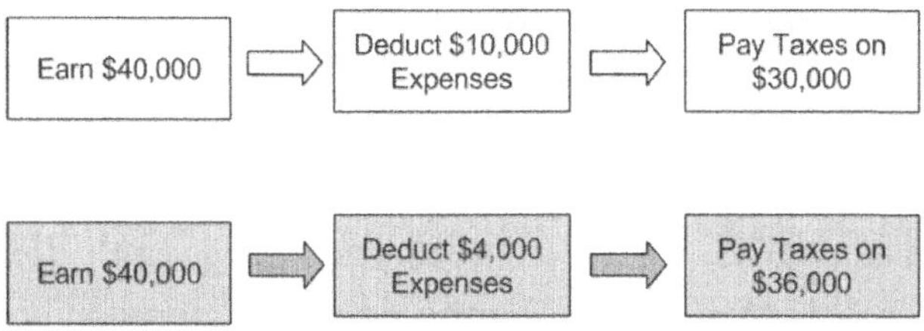

Chart Showing Example Deductions from a $40,000 Income

Section 199A Deduction

As part of the new Tax Cuts & Jobs Act (TCJA), there is an additional deduction specifically for pass-through businesses (sole proprietorships, LLCs, S Corps and Partnerships). Section 199A provides a 20% reduction of Qualified Business Income (QBI) for these types of entities. Since this is a new deduction, interpreters should expect further clarification and regulations to be released over the years.

If you qualify for this deduction, you would simply subtract an additional 20% from your net qualified business income and pay taxes on the new net income amount. In Example

1, instead of paying taxes on $30,000 net business income, you would instead pay taxes on $24,000 ($30,000 – 20%= $24,000). In Example 2 instead of paying taxes on $36,000 net business income, you would instead pay taxes on $28,800 ($36,000 – 20%= $28,800). This offers a huge tax savings for those who qualify.

According to IRS Revenue Procedure 2018-57, in order to qualify for the Qualified Business Income Deduction, your taxable income must be less than $160,700 if you're single, or less than $321,400 if you are married filing jointly. If you earn more than these thresholds, there are additional stipulations to determine eligibility status. Since a majority of freelance interpreters earn below these thresholds, we will not discuss additional stipulations in this book.

Additional details on this provision and other major TCJA changes are explained in plain language by Ronald Mueller in his book, "America's New 2018 Tax Cuts and Jobs Act". This is a 54-page executive summary geared towards helping everyday taxpayers comprehend the 53 most significant tax changes now in effect.

Business Expense Deductions

The IRS says that your deductible expenses must be "both ordinary and necessary" for business operations. These kinds of expenses are only deductible if and when the business is operating to make a profit. It is easy to get confused by what items can be deducted. For example, the IRS says that you cannot deduct personal, living, or family expenses. But if any given expense is partly used for your business and partly used for personal use, you can divide the total cost between the business and personal use. Simply put, you can only deduct the portion of any expense that went directly toward the maintenance of your business.

For example, many interpreters use the same phone for both personal and business use. If 50% of your phone use is for business, and 50% is for personal use, then you can divide the cost between legitimate business use and personal (nondeductible) use. In this case, if my phone bill is $100/month then I can deduct $50/month as a business expense.

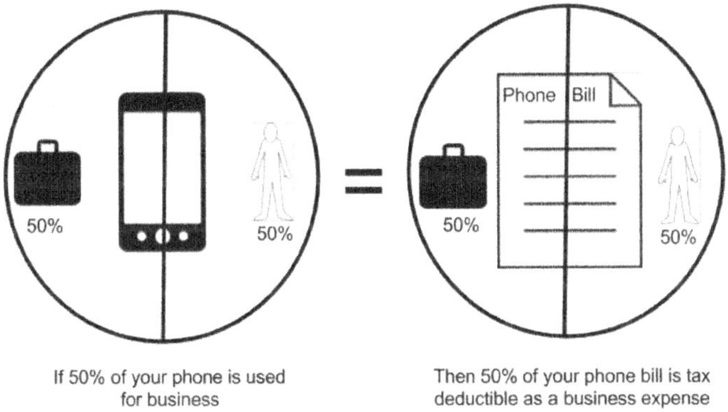

Division of telephone expenses between business and personal use

Not surprisingly, a W-2 employed interpreter and a sole proprietor interpreter have different kinds of allowable deductions. For the most part, the sole proprietor has an opportunity to deduct more of their expenses than the W-2 employee. The IRS gives self-employed individuals this opportunity because they don't have an employer to cover business expenses such as office space, equipment and health insurance.

Even the IRS tax forms filled out by sole proprietors and W-2 employees are different. At the end of the year the sole proprietor files a Schedule C or C-EZ, which is the profit and loss form showing their deductible expenses. The W-2 employee does not fill out a Schedule C and does not qualify for the same deductions as an independent contractor. Many freelance interpreters lose money on their taxes by assuming that they cannot take certain deductions. In this chapter we will give you a basic knowledge of some deductions so you can take advantage of these money saving opportunities.

Start-up Cost Deductions

When you initially start your interpreting business there are deduction opportunities right out of the gate. However, you must meet the IRS's criteria in order to qualify certain expenses as true 'start-up costs'. The Internal Revenue website, IRS.gov, states, "start-up costs are amounts paid or incurred for (a) creating an active trade or business, or

(b) investigating the creation or acquisition of an active trade or business."

Once your expenses meet these criteria as allowable start-up deductions, you will be required to categorize them. Some are general business start-up costs, organizational start-up costs or business assets. An example of some general business start-up costs may include advertising, travel, supplies used for meeting with customers, business or finance training before the business actually begins, and so on. Organizational costs may include LLC formation fees, business license fees, attorney consultations etc. Business assets may include business cars, equipment, office furniture or other assets that have a lifespan of over one year.

Example Deductions		
Start-up Costs	**Organizational Costs**	**Business Asset/Capital Expense**
Advertising, travel, supplies used for meeting customers, business/finance training before the business actually begins, etc.	LLC formation fees, business license fees, attorney consultations, etc.	Business cars, equipment, office furniture or other expensive assets that have a lifespan of over one year

Examples of Deductions:
Start-up vs. Organizational vs. Business Assets

START-UP COSTS & ORGANIZATIONAL COST DEDUCTIONS

The IRS allows you to deduct, as of 2019, up to $5,000 in business start-up costs and an additional $5,000 in organizational costs before you start your business. So, if you become a business entity, you would be able to utilize $10,000 worth of approved deductions for start-up and organizational costs. If you become a sole proprietor, you wouldn't need the additional $5,000 deduction allowed for organizational costs because there are no entity formation expenses.

If your start-up costs are more than $5,000, you can still write off a portion of the remaining cost by prorating it over the next 180 months (15 years). This is called amortization. This is also assuming your start-up costs are less than $50,000. If your costs are more than $50,000, please ask an attorney or tax professional for guidance.

Let's look at an example. If you are starting out as a sole proprietor and your start-up costs are $10,000, you can write off the allowed $5,000 on your first year's taxes. The remaining $5,000 can be amortized over a 180-month period, which provides you with a running deduction of around $27 a month for the next fifteen years. Your annual amortization deduction would thus be around $333 per year.

You spent $10,000 in startup costs this year.

$5,000 is tax-deductible start-up costs.

$5,000 is amortized (spread out) over 180 months. Each year $333 is tax deductible ($27/month).

How to Deduct Startup Costs for a Sole Proprietorship

Business Asset or Capital Expense Deductions

These capital expenses are treated differently than your ordinary operating expenses such as salaries, rent, travel, etc. Rather, expenses that are made to purchase business assets, also known as capital expenditures, can be depreciated over a period of time. As mentioned above, this process of deducting the cost of an item over a long period of time is called amortization. The cost of amortized items is prorated over the expected lifetime of the piece of equipment in question. This type of deduction applies to more expensive business asset expenses, such as a car. For less expensive business assets, the amount may be too insignificant to amortize. Therefore, these less expensive business assets can simply be deducted as business expenses, not as capital expenses.

In the first year after purchasing expensive business assets you can take a portion of the cost as a deduction and then spread the rest of the cost out over a number of years. There are also deductions for intangible, or nonphysical, expenses such as computer software. Under certain circumstances you may be eligible for a Section 179 deduction, which would allow you to write these normally amortized deductions off in the same year in which they were incurred. For more information on Section 179 deductions, please consult a tax professional.

As a side note, Sandy Botkin, who is a CPA and former IRS attorney, states that if the office in your home fails to qualify for the home office deduction because it is also used for personal use, you still can depreciate the office furniture and equipment that you use for business purposes. If you end up using it 80% of the time for work, the chair, computer, and other work-related items may be depreciated.

Standard Mileage vs. Actual Car Cost Deduction

When it comes to your car, there are only two methods of deduction you can pick from: the standard mileage rate or actual car expenses. Please consult a tax professional to find out which method is the best fit for your situation.

Actual Car Expense Method

The actual car expense deduction allows you to deduct the following items from your taxes: gas, oil changes, tolls, repairs, maintenance, lease payments, insurance, registration fees, parking fees, tires, garage rent, etc. But bear in mind that you are not allowed to deduct any mileage under this option. If you choose to depreciate your car, you will be required to stay with this method for the lifespan of the car.

Standard Mileage Method

The standard mileage-rate deduction is an IRS approved rate that business owners use to deduct the number of business miles they drive in a given year. This annual mileage amount (the IRS approved rate multiplied by business miles) is deductible at the end of the year. You can also deduct registration fees, parking, tolls and interest on car loans under this option. This deduction amount is subject to how much you use your car for business. Automobile registration fees vary by state and are only deductible if the fees are based on the value of the car (personal property tax). Lastly, you are not allowed to deduct any vehicle expenses from the Actual Car Expense Method (above) under this option except those specifically noted. If you choose the Standard Mileage Method the first year the car is used, you are allowed to switch to the Actual Car Expense Method in future years. Once you make the switch, however, you will have to stay with the Actual Car Expense Method for the life of the car if you start depreciating.

	Actual Car Expense Method	Standard Mileage Method
Expenses you CAN deduct	Gas, oil changes, tolls, repairs, maintenance, lease payments, insurance, registration fees, parking fees, tires, garage rent, etc.	The annual mileage amount (the IRS approved rate multiplied by your business miles), registration fees, parking, tolls and interest on car loans, etc.
Expenses you CAN NOT deduct	Mileage.	Any vehicle expenses from the Actual Car Expense Method.
Things to consider when choosing a method	If you choose to depreciate your car, then you need to stay with this method for the life of the car.	If you choose this method the first year the car is used, you are allowed to switch to actual car expense method in future years.

Actual Car Expense Method vs. Standard Mileage Deduction

HOW MUCH TO DEDUCT

You can only deduct the percentage of auto related expenses that are directly related to business. For example, many interpreters use their car for both business AND personal travel. Let's say an interpreter chooses the Actual Car Expense Method. If they only use their car for business around 30% of the time, then they can only deduct 30% of their vehicle expenses. If this same interpreter had to do $1000 worth of car repairs, they would only deduct $300 (30% of $1,000) on their taxes. You can determine your percent of business use by tracking your miles (regardless of which method you choose). By tracking your miles on a log (your mileage, date, destination, purpose) you can calculate how much of your car usage was for business in the tax year. There are many apps available, 'Mile IQ' for example, that can help you keep a mileage log digitally. A physical notebook also works well as long as you're diligent with record keeping (see Chapter 4).

In general, the standard mileage method is easier because all you need is the previously described mileage log. In order to use the actual expense method, you need a mileage log along with additional receipts for all expenses you intend to deduct. A mileage log is necessary for both methods because it is used to show your percent of business usage.

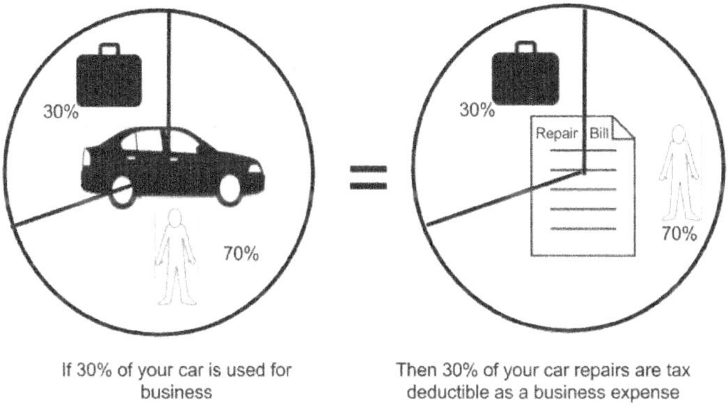

Example Car Expenses as they Relate to Tax Deductions

Travel

Your daily travel expenses can be deducted as long as they are "ordinary" and "necessary" expenses that are common in your business field and meet home office requirements. In order to understand travel deductions as it applies to your commute, we must first discuss the home office. Freelance interpreters often travel to and from their assignments from home. To understand which commutes are tax-deductible, we must know whether or not an established home office is in place.

Working without an Established Home Office

The IRS states that you cannot deduct any travel costs while commuting to and from your home. As a freelance interpreter, according to the IRS, the location of your first job of the day is considered your temporary office. The commute from your home to your first job (i.e. your temporary office) is NOT deductible. However, if you have a second assignment afterwards, the cost of travel from your first job (temporary office) to the second job IS deductible. The travel cost from your second assignment back to your home is NOT deductible. Additionally, even if the IRS determines your first place of business to be your 'corporate headquarters' (temporary office), traveling to meet with your interpreting team or business prospect or pick up supplies is also considered to be business mileage.

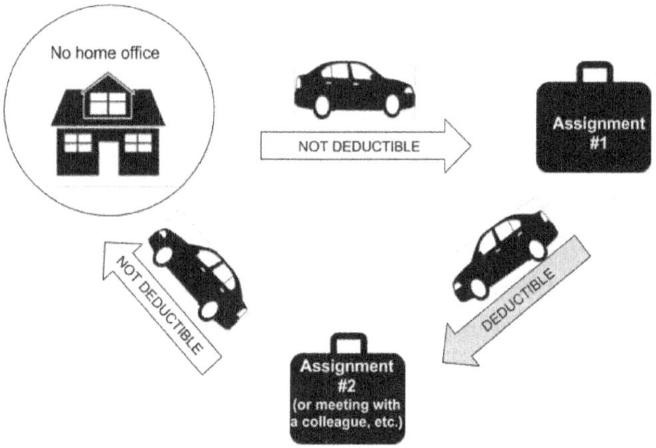

Travel Deductions without a Formally Established Home Office

Working with an Established Home Office

If your home office is your official headquarters you should be able to deduct the travel cost of the commute to your first job of the day. This is allowed as long as administrative and management tasks take place in your home office. In essence, you can deduct the round trip to and from your assignments if you have formally established a home office. To find out if you qualify, please refer to the home office section of this chapter and the following chart to learn about what constitutes a home office.

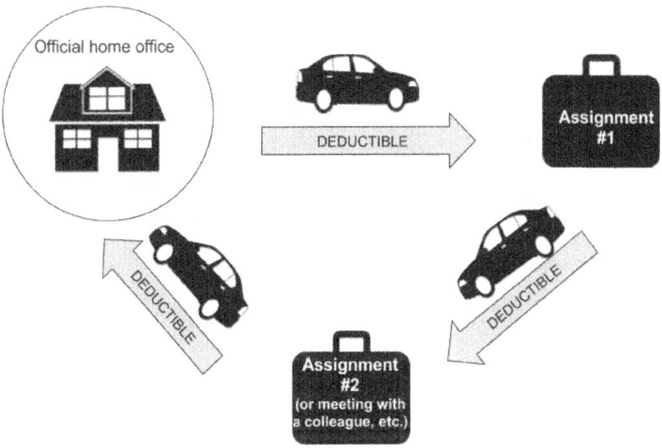

Travel Deductions with a Formally Established Home Office

Working out of State

If you accept an interpreting assignment out of state, or overseas, even if it is just to meet with a client or a support professional, you are still eligible for travel deductions as long as your trip expenses meet the requirements of "ordinary" and "necessary" business expenses. The IRS recommends that you keep all records relating to business expenses. This can be accomplished by keeping some kind of log, notebook, diary or any other system that helps you track the expenses incurred on your trip (see Chapter 4).

Feel free to use the following IRS travel deduction table as a quick reference to what basic business travel deductions are available.

Travel Expenses You Can Deduct

The following chart summarizes expenses you can deduct when you travel away from home for business purposes.

IF you have expenses for...	THEN you can deduct the cost of...
Transportation	Travel by airplane, train, bus, or car between your home and your business destination. If you were provided with a free ticket, or you are riding free as a result of a frequent traveler or similar program, your cost is zero. If you travel by ship, see Luxury Water Travel and Cruise Ships (under Conventions) for additional rules and limits.
Taxi, commuter bus, and airport limousine	Fares for these and other types of transportation that take you between: The airport or station and your hotel, and the hotel and the work location of your customers or clients, your business meeting place, or your temporary work location.
Baggage and shipping	Sending baggage or display material between your regular and temporary work locations.

Car	Operating and maintaining your car when traveling away from home on business. You can deduct actual expenses or the standard mileage rate, as well as business related tolls and parking. If you rent a car while away from home on business, you can deduct only the business-use portion of the expenses.
Lodging and meals	Your lodging and meals if your business trip is overnight or long enough that you need to stop for sleep or rest to properly perform your duties. Meals include amounts spent for food, beverages, taxes, and related tips. See Meals for additional rules and limits.
Cleaning	Dry cleaning and laundry.
Telephone	Business calls while on your business trip. This includes business communication by fax machine or other communication devices.
Tips	Tips you pay for any expenses in this chart.

Other	Other similar ordinary and necessary expenses related to your business travel. These expenses might include transportation to or from a business meal, public stenographer's fees, computer rental fees, and operating and maintaining a house trailer.

IRS Publication 463 Travel, Gift, and Car Expenses

Home office deduction

The IRS has requirements if you intend to qualify your home office as a deductible expense. The portion of the home used as an office must exclusively be used for conducting business. You are allowed to have a home office even if it's just for administrative or management activities. This is helpful for interpreters because our work is often conducted outside of the home. You must be able to prove that your home office is used as the principal place of business. Which means it needs to be a separate space with a desk and computer. The space cannot include personal items like a bed. In addition, you must keep the activities performed in your home office business related. So don't do laundry or have a movie night in your home office.

Regular Method

The home office tax deduction is based on the percentage of your home that is used for business purposes. This method gives you the ability to deduct actual expenses that apply to your home office. These expenses may include mortgage interest, insurance, utilities, repairs and depreciation. When using the regular method, you calculate the percentage or the square footage of the whole area that is dedicated for business use. That would be the percentage used for determining how much to deduct. To do this, divide the square footage of the office by the total square footage of your home. To illustrate, a 250 square foot office in a 2,500 square foot home yields a business percentage use of 10% (see the following figure).

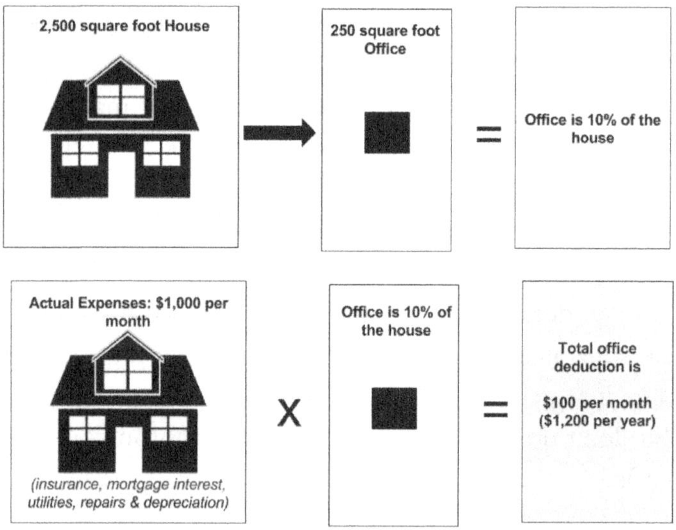

Office Deduction Example Scenario: Regular Method
(actual expenses x percent of business use)

SIMPLIFIED METHOD

The other possible method you can use is called the Simplified Method. This option is used in lieu of keeping track of the actual home office expenses that you would normally record in the Regular Method, thus, making it 'simple' and less burdensome for a small business. In this method, you simply multiply $5 by the square footage of your office (maximum 300 square feet). To illustrate, a 250 square foot office in a 2,500 square foot home yields a business deduction of $1,250 per year (250 sq ft x $5 = $1,250). With this method you won't be able to deduct depreciation or any other home office deductions.

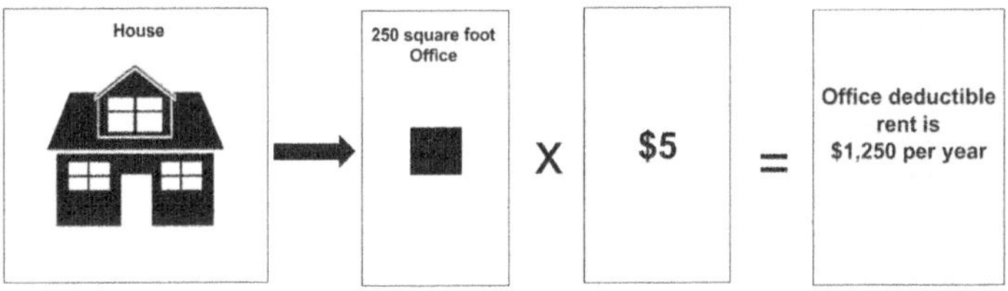

Office Deduction Example Scenario: Simplified Method

Comparison of Methods

<table>
<tr><th>Simplified Option</th><th>Regular Method</th></tr>
<tr><td colspan="2">Deduction for home office located in a portion of a residence is allowed only if that portion is exclusively used on a regular basis for business purposes.</td></tr>
<tr><td>Allowable square footage of home used for business (not to exceed 300 square feet).</td><td>Percentage of home used for business.</td></tr>
<tr><td>Standard $5 per square foot used to determine home business deduction.</td><td>Actual expenses determined and records maintained.</td></tr>
<tr><td>Home-related expenses cannot be itemized.</td><td>Home-related itemized deductions listed on Schedule C.</td></tr>
<tr><td>No depreciation deduction.</td><td>Depreciation deduction for portion of home used for business.</td></tr>
<tr><td>No recapture of depreciation upon sale of home.</td><td>Recapture of depreciation on gain upon sale of home.</td></tr>
<tr><td colspan="2">Deduction cannot exceed gross income from business use of home, less business expenses.</td></tr>
</table>

Amount in excess of gross income limitation may <u>not</u> be carried over.	Amount in excess of gross income limitation may be carried over.
Loss carryover from use of regular method in prior year may <u>not</u> be claimed.	Loss carryover from use of regular method in prior year may be claimed if gross income test is met in the current year.

Office Deductions: Simplified vs. Regular Method

The IRS has publications online that describe which deductions you qualify for. If you are a homeowner planning on deducting your home office, it is strongly encouraged that you consult with a tax professional first. If a homeowner deducts home office expenses, it can potentially inhibit their ability to avoid capital gains tax when selling the primary residence.

Meals

The IRS offers general rules for meal deductions. The IRS states, "The meal must be business related." You can deduct 50% of business meals with a client, vendor, or partner for the sole purpose of discussing business. When traveling out of town, you can deduct 50% of meals even when eating by yourself. Basically, in order to deduct 50% of local meals, you must be with someone and discussing business. The only time you can deduct a meal when you're alone is if you are out of town on business.

Conclusion

Understanding what deductions are available to you can help offset the taxes you will owe each quarter or at the end of the year. Obviously, this section could not go into detail on every single deduction available (like professional development, office supplies, software, etc.), but we hope it gave you a general sense of some of the deductions you can take as freelance interpreters. Always keep in mind which deductions give you the most bang for your buck. For example, travel is 100% deductible while meals are only 50% deductible. Also keep in mind that business deductions are not the only deductions you will encounter when filing taxes. There are also personal tax deductions like standard vs. itemized deductions reported on Schedule A (visit www.IRS.gov for details). In the next chapter we will discuss how to keep track of these deductible business expenses by saving receipts or using bookkeeping software.

CHAPTER MAIN POINTS

- Key Concept: Save money by using business expense deductions.
- Business deductions are ONLY for business expenses. If an item is used for business 50% of the time, only deduct 50% of its cost or running expense.

Start-up Cost Deductions: $10,000		
Start-up Cost	**Organizational Cost**	**Capital Expense**
$5,000 allowed.	$5,000 allowed. Not applicable for Sole Proprietors.	Expensive assets depreciated over life span of the item.

Car Deductions	
Actual Car Expense Method	**Standard Mileage Method**
CAN deduct gas, oil change, lease, insurance, etc. CANNOT deduct mileage.	CAN deduct mileage. CANNOT deduct expenses from Actual Car Expense Method.

Traveling		
With Home Office	**Without Home Office**	**Working out of State**
CAN deduct round trip to and from home.	CAN deduct commute in-between jobs. CANNOT deduct commute to and from home.	CAN deduct travel expenses (see table).

Home Office Deduction	
Regular Method	**Simplified Method**
Based on the percent of house used for the office.	Multiply $5 by the square footage of your office.

Meals
50% of the cost is deductible if with colleagues or clients for business matters locally. For traveling out of town, eating alone is acceptable.

TAKE ACTION!

1. Start-up costs I plan on deducting:

☐ Advertising
☐ Travel
☐ Supplies used for meeting customers
☐ Business/finance training before the business actually begins
☐ Other: ____________

2. Organizational costs I plan on deducting (not applicable for sole proprietors):

☐ LLC formation fees
☐ Business license fees
☐ CPA fees
☐ Attorney consultations
☐ Other: ____________

3. Business asset/Capital expenses I plan on deducting:

☐ Business cars
☐ Expensive equipment/office furniture
☐ Other: ____________

4. If you have a car, choose which expense method you will use this year:

☐ Actual car expense method
☐ Standard mileage method

5. Do you have a formally established home office?

- ☐ Yes
- ☐ No

6. Based on your answer, are you allowed to deduct your commute in-between jobs and to and from home?

- ☐ Yes
- ☐ No

7. If you have a formally established home office, choose which deduction method you will use this year:

- ☐ Regular method
- ☐ Simplified method

8. Here are other common business expense deductions that interpreters may have. Check off any that you think you might have this year.

☐ Professional Development *(interpreting related workshops, conferences and books)*

☐ Business use of phone

☐ Licenses *(certification or membership fees)*

☐ Office Supplies *(pens, paper, ink, etc)*

☐ Business Public Transportation *(follows same rules as auto deduction. Visit this section for details)*

CHAPTER 4: BOOKKEEPING

The goal of bookkeeping is to keep you and your business financially organized. Proper bookkeeping is a great way to stay on target with your business and financial goals. It also helps you maintain the documentation necessary to justify your deductible expenses in case of an audit. Luckily there are many tools interpreters can use to streamline their bookkeeping and finances.

Banking

The first step in handling your bookkeeping is to separate your personal and business finances. If you become an LLC or an LLC S Corp, opening a business checking account is one way to do this. After you have filed paperwork for your business as an LLC, you will need to take your articles, operating agreement and your EIN (Employer Identification Number) to the bank of your choice to open a business account.

If you choose to remain a sole proprietor, simply opening up a second checking account under your personal name will be sufficient in the beginning because sole proprietorships do not require any formal business paperwork. If you, as a sole proprietor, prefer a business checking account, creating a trade name/DBA (Doing Business As) and getting an EIN will allow you to do so.

The important thing to remember is keep your business and personal expenses separate. If you keep your business and personal expenses 100% separate it will legitimize your business as well as make it much easier to track your tax deductions. Even getting a debit card, in which you designate for business use only, can help because you can pull your monthly statements to keep up with your business expenses.

Bookkeeping 101

Bookkeeping is designed to provide business owners a quick and efficient way to record all of their financial related activities. In other words, keeping track of purchases, invoices, payroll, and basically any financial transactions that impact the business. Setting up a bookkeeping system is the first step in keeping your 'books' organized for your accounting. When filing your taxes at the end of the year, or even in the event of an audit, all your records will depend on how organized your bookkeeping practices are. A tax professional can also help you establish good bookkeeping practices. If you are already interpreting and haven't created any type of bookkeeping structure, there are plenty of bookkeeping programs to help you get organized.

Accounting Methods: Cash vs. Accrual

When setting up a bookkeeping system, interpreters will need to choose between two systems known as cash accounting and accrual accounting.

Cash accounting means that money is only recorded when it is actually received and the cash shows up in your bank account. The same is true of expenses; they aren't recognized and recorded until you pay your expenses and the cash comes out of your account.

For example, let's say you send a $500 invoice on January 1st, and the company pays you on February 1st. If you followed a cash accounting system, you would document that payment as being received February 1st. Cash accounting may seem simpler because income and expenses are only recorded as they happen. Here is a more specific example: In December of this year, you decide that you'd like to attend an interpreting conference, but the event happens in January of following year. In this case, the cost of the conference would count as an expense in the year in which you paid for it, not in the year in which it happened. Similarly, if you invoiced a client in December but got paid in January, the amount would be counted as income for the year in which you got paid, not the year in which you sent out the invoice.

Accrual accounting, on the other hand, is when your bookkeeping follows the dates of your invoices. For example: if you send a $500 invoice on January 1st, and the company pays you on February 1st, you would document the earnings on January 1st. Your account will show an increase in revenue on January 1st even though your bank account doesn't reflect the increased balance. The same goes for expenses, which are also accounted for at the time they are accrued instead of when you actually pay the bill.

Example Scenario:
You send an invoice for \$500 on January 1st.
Payment is due February 1st.

Cash Accounting:
The \$500 is documented as revenue when the cash is received in your bank account.

Accrual Accounting:
The \$500 is documented as revenue when the invoice is sent.

Cash vs. Accrual Accounting Example

Having a budget will help you keep track of how much you are spending and ensure you can afford your planned expenses without creating a deficit. It is recommended that businesses selling products or have inventory use the accrual method, but freelance interpreters typically don't have inventory so a simple cash accounting system should be sufficient. Please consult your tax professional to discuss which method fits your financial situation and business operations.

Bookkeeping Software

Although it is important to have a general grasp on bookkeeping concepts, there are ways to make things easier on you as a freelancer. One way is by using online software. We recommend a widely used system called QuickBooks. It allows the average person to do their own bookkeeping by making the above concepts into a user-friendly system. QuickBooks also comes with asset, liability, and expense account ledgers ready for use.

You can download the online version of systems like QuickBooks for a monthly payment or purchase the software and install it directly into your computer. Choose whichever method works best for you. There are advantages and disadvantages to all accounting software. In this book, we will only be discussing the features of QuickBooks Online (QBO). For more information about QuickBooks' other systems, please visit QuickBooks.com. Keep in mind that there are programs, such as Zoho, Sage One, FreshBooks Cloud Accounting, Xero, etc., that may also suit your needs.

Record Keeping

It is important to keep track of your expenses in case the IRS audits you. Not only should you keep track of receipts or transactions (such as in QuickBooks) but also include some extra details to prove that the expense is business related. Keeping track of who, what, where, when, the purpose, etc. can be of substantial help if you experience an audit. In QuickBooks, you can open up your expense transaction and include extra details in the memo section.

This is a great way to avoid carrying a notebook around with you every time you have to log an expense.

An Interpreting Related Business Expense May Look Something Like This:

Business Expense Record: On ________(date) at __________(time), I had a lunch meeting at ___________(name of place) with my co-interpreter, __________________(co-interpreter's first and last name), to talk about the details of our interpreting assignment.

Example Interpreting Business Expense Record

Please consult with your tax preparer on how they would like you to record/log your expenses. See the following table as a reference when documenting the details of your business expenses.

IF you have expenses for:	**THEN you must keep records that show details of the following elements:**			
	Amount	Time	Description	Business Purpose
Travel	Cost of each separate expense for travel, lodging, and meals. Incidental expenses may be totaled in reasonable categories such as taxis, fees and tips, etc.	Dates you left and returned for each trip and number of days spent on business.	Destination or area of your travel (name of city, town, or other designation).	Business purpose for the expense or the business benefit gained or expected to be gained.
Transportation	Cost of each separate expense. For car expenses, the cost of the car and any improvements, the date you started using it for business, the mileage for each business use, and the total miles for the year.	Date of the expense. For car expenses, the date of the use of the car.	Your business destination.	Business purpose for the expense.

IRS Publication 463: How to Prove Certain Business Expenses

Chart of Accounts

QBO syncs with your bank account and tracks every transaction you make. Thanks to this feature you can go into the system and label each transaction as an asset, liability, owner's equity, revenue, or expense. A chart of accounts, in the bookkeeping sense, is your business's formal index of categories that help you track financial transactions. By staying up to date on your transactions and labeling them correctly, you will have immediate access to many different types of reports that will show you where your money is going. This can also be very helpful at the end of the year when you, or your tax preparer, needs to see what tax deductions you have. Instead of just having a box of receipts you will have everything you need, neatly arranged, in digital format.

Budgeting

Budgeting can be done in many different ways. There is no right or wrong approach to establishing a budget, so feel free to experiment. John A. Tracy, who is a professor of accounting at the University of Colorado and the author of *Accounting for Dummies*, explains that a budget is a statement of transactions based on future expectations. Basically, a budget categorizes your predictions of what you will be spending and earning. Setting up a budget will help you avoid overspending. You can create a budget for the year, quarter, or for the month while maintaining a little flexibility for any unforeseen changes. Having a budget can also help you keep track of paying your quarterly taxes and how much to contribute to your retirement fund(s).

How to Stay within a Personal Budget

One approach to budgeting is to set up a personal monthly budget for different categories of spending. For example, maybe you spend $400 a month on food, your rent is $800, your gym membership is $30, your phone bill is $80, etc. Creating an initial budget may be pretty easy, but the real challenge arises when you have to follow it. Here are some different approaches to staying within your budget.

One option is using a simple spreadsheet. You can type out categories and make a budget from scratch or download one of the many free templates online. The only problem with using a spreadsheet is that you have to manually update it as you spend. This can become cumbersome and it's easy to fall behind.

Luckily, we live in an age of limitless technology. There are many apps and software packages that can help streamline your budgeting system. 'You Need a Budget' (YNAB) is a great online system that allows you to establish monthly budgets and move funds around accordingly as you over or under spend. The best part about this particular software is the additional resources. There are ample videos and blogs with tips and strategies, not only on how to budget effectively, but also how to pay off debt. The only downfall to this program is that after a 34-day free trial it costs $50 annually. For more information, check out www.youneedabudget.com.

If you are looking for a simpler, and cost-free budgeting software, Mint (Mint.com) is a great one. It allows you to create budgets and syncs up with your bank accounts just like YNAB. Dave Ramsey, a well-known author on money management offers a software called 'Every Dollar' (DaveRamsey.com/EveryDollar). It's similar to YNAB and is free with an optional paid upgrade. Another option is to find out if your bank provides any budgeting software. These are not the only apps and software out there, so enjoy shopping around and reading reviews before making a decision. The software, or system, you choose is solely based on personal preference.

Once a personal monthly budget has been created you can use these numbers to guide you to establishing an emergency fund. For those who work as self-employed individuals, Dave Ramsey recommends saving up to 6 months' worth of monthly expenses. Freelance interpreters might have weeks or months where work is slow (summer time or holidays) and an emergency fund can be there to help cover those unexpected financial moments. In addition to an emergency fund, it would behoove an interpreter to also build a business budget to save for future business expenses such as transportation, professional development, office expenses and etc.

Using Budgets to Guide your Freelance Schedule

Once a personal monthly budget has been created you can use these numbers to guide you when scheduling interpreting jobs.

Here is one approach for using your personal budget to organize your freelance schedule:

1. Figure out how much money you need monthly to personally survive (i.e. create your initial budget). Include rent, utilities, food budget, transportation, retirement, fun money, etc. (i.e. $2500).

2. You'll need to save for self-employment tax and income taxes, so add these to your expenses in your budget. For most interpreters, 20%-30% is a safe amount to set aside for taxes.

3. Once you know how much your monthly expenses are (i.e. $3,250), divide that number by your freelance rate, which we have arbitrarily set at $45.00 per hour. Your formula for the month is therefore $3250 ÷ $45= 72 hours. To meet your basic personal expenses, you will need to work 72 hours that month.

4. Now, divide this number, 72, by 4 to see how many hours you need to work per week:
$72 \div 4 = 18$ hours a week.

In this scenario you need a minimum of 18 hours per week to support your living expenses. With this information, you can now book your time accordingly.

This approach can take a lot of stress out of scheduling yourself. It can be very tempting to work all day everyday just because you can. But if you get injured, or need to take time off, this approach can be helpful in making sure you can at least cover your personal expenses. By knowing the minimum number of hours you need to work per month, you can book yourself more strategically and avoid over/under working.

Conclusion

Organization is key to keeping your budget, and your business, on track. Finding a bookkeeping system that works for you is crucial. We recommend that you separate your business and personal finances, familiarize yourself with basic bookkeeping concepts, budgeting and, if desired, set up a bookkeeping software system, as soon as possible. Once you become comfortable with your personal budget, you can choose to create a completely separate business budget. By getting these items in place your business will be able to run much more smoothly, especially during tax season. Tax professionals and bookkeepers have the most expertise on keeping this part of your business life in balance. Take advantage of the resources and support available to you!

CHAPTER MAIN POINTS

- Key Concept: Stay organized and separate business and personal finances.
- Banking
  - Separate your business and personal finances.

Accounting 101	
Cash Accounting	**Accrual Accounting**
Document money as you receive/spend it.	Document money following the invoice/billing date.

- Record Keeping
  - Keep track of your expenses with detail in the event an audit happens.
- Bookkeeping Software
  - A Chart of Accounts keeps your expenses organized for tax deductions.
  - Profit and loss reports can provide you with 'the big picture' of how you are doing financially.
  - Keep track of your business expenses in case the IRS audits you.

Use a Budget to Guide your Schedule (example)	
Steps	**What to do**
1	Monthly expenses (including extra to cover taxes): $3,250.
2	Divide this number by your freelance rate: $3250/ $45 = 72 hours per month.
3	Divide this number by 4: 72/4 = you need to work at least 18 hours per week to cover your spending habits.

- Creating a System: How to Stay within Budget
    - Manual: Spreadsheets
    - Paid Systems:
        - YouNeedABudget.com
    - Free Systems:
        - Mint.com
        - DaveRamsey.com/Everydollar

TAKE ACTION!

1. How will you separate your business and personal expenses?

☐ I will choose one credit card to use for business expenses.

☐ I will open a new personal checking account for business expenses.

☐ I will open a business checking account for business expenses.

☐ Other: ____________

2. Which accounting method will you use?

☐ I will use cash accounting.

☐ I will use accrual accounting.

3. What bookkeeping software will you use?

☐ QuickBooks

☐ Zoho

☐ Sage One

☐ Freshbooks Cloud Accounting

☐ Xero

☐ Other: ____________

4. Let's set up your budget together!

My monthly expenses are:
$________

My hourly rate is:
$___________

How many hours I need work per month:
(Monthly expenses divided by hourly rate)
________/ ________ =__________

How many hours I need to work per week:
(Hours I need to work per month divided by 4)
________ / = ____________

I need to work at least __________hours per week to cover my spending habits

5. What is your budgeting system?

- ☐ Manual: Spreadsheets
- ☐ You Need A Budget
- ☐ Mint
- ☐ Every Dollar
- ☐ Other: _______________

Chapter 5: Business Practices

Interpreters often begin their career living paycheck to paycheck, scheduling assignments with a simple calendar and taking each situation as it comes. Although this is perfectly fine in the beginning, it will pay off in the long run to eventually develop some consistent business practices. Viewing yourself as your own small business may seem odd at first, especially if your business only involves you, interpreting every day, and then coming home to go about your life. But by embracing a business owner mindset you will start to see areas of your work life that could become more efficient.

Getting Organized

Doing your own scheduling is more than just booking interpreting assignments; it's a lifestyle. Freelance interpreters can have a well thought-out calendar system, not only to keep track of assignments but also to track 'to do' items, personal obligations, invoicing, etc. A wonderful book to read about organization is *Getting Things Done* by David Allen. In his book, Allen discusses a simple way of organizing your life by considering everything, from planning your next vacation to invoicing customers, as an action item. He explains a system of organizing these action items in a way that will ensure you never forget them again. From his perspective, trying to remember and hold on to information in our heads causes stress and anxiety, and is also a huge waste of energy. The process discussed in *Getting Things Done* is fairly in depth, so for the sake of this book, we will only discuss one small piece: tasks that require action on your part (see the following figure).

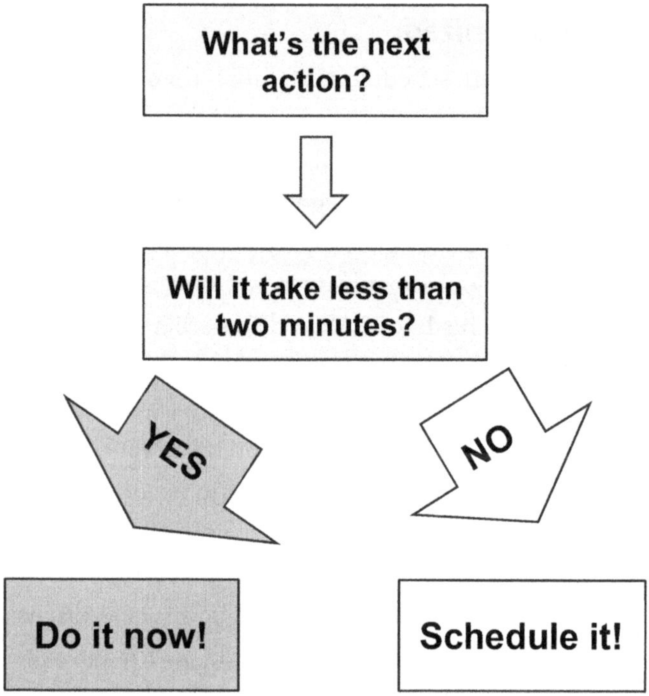

"Getting Things Done" Process for Tasks that Require Action

If there is something you need to get done, ask yourself the following questions: What is the next action? Will that action take less than 2 minutes? If yes, complete the action now. If it takes longer than 2 minutes, schedule it for a later date when you have the time to complete it. See the following figures for examples specific to the interpreting field.

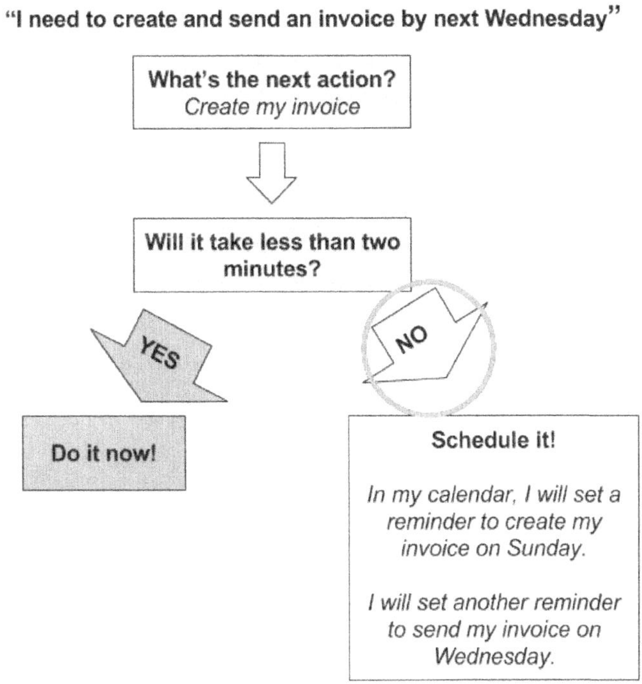

Getting Things Done Example Scenario: Invoicing

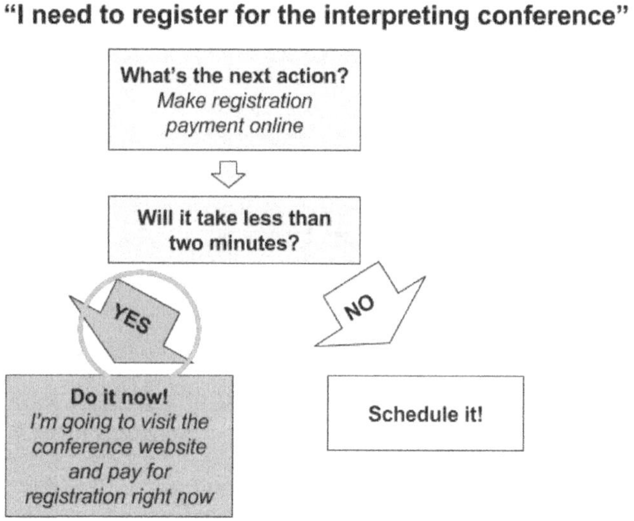

Getting Things Done Example Scenario: Conference Registration

By applying David Allen's basic principles, you will be able to set up a system that works for your particular lifestyle. Once you've decided on an organizational strategy that works for you, there are many systems and apps that can assist in keeping you on top of your daily routine.

Calendar & Task Apps

Having a clear list of prioritized tasks will be helpful in staying organized. 'Pocket Informant' is a great app that combines both your calendar items and to do items into one place. With Pocket Informant you can also color code different days to indicate different things. For example, yellow might mean that you still need to find work for that day, orange might mean that you have tentative work for that day, blue might mean that you're taking off that day, and so on.

Evernote (www.evernote.com) is another well-known software that can be used for to do items. You can create a new note for each task you have to complete, assign it a due date and attach any relevant information to that note to make completing the task easier.

Trello (www.trello.com) is a more visual organization software. Each project or category resembles a board. And each to do item on that board resembles a post it note (or what they call cards). In your project, you can create columns at the top of the board that say "to do", "working on" and "done". Then you can drag these tasks from column to column as you complete them.

Another more advanced organizational software is Asana (www.asana.com). Although there's a bit of a learning curve, once mastered, it can be a great way to implement the *Getting Things Done* model. You can create different projects for the different areas of your life and create associated tasks. In each task you can upload documents, images, etc. to help you accomplish important jobs quickly. You can also assign due dates to important projects. Although this may appear to be similar to Evernote and

Trello, the main difference is that it includes multiple view options. In Asana you can see your tasks in a month-to-month view like a calendar, in a list view like Evernote, or a board view like Trello.

These are merely recommendations that only scratch the surface of what's available. Everyday new productivity apps are being released into the market. Any calendar or to do list app can work fine as long as you're able to rely on it. Shop around and enjoy experimenting with what works best for you.

Emails

Receiving an endless series of emails from agencies describing the type of jobs that are available can become overwhelming. Keeping an organized email inbox is a great way to make sure you don't double book yourself or overlook a job confirmation. Most email accounts (Gmail, Outlook, Yahoo, etc.) have the option to create folders. Consider a simple folder system to keep track of jobs you don't want, jobs you are awaiting confirmation for and jobs you are confirmed for.

A more efficient approach that's commonly available is the use of filters. Filters allow you to automatically put certain emails in specific folders the moment they arrive to you. In Gmail, there is even an option to have these select emails skip your inbox and go straight into their designated folder.

By using this feature, you could create a folder for each interpreting agency in your region; and then create a filter so that emails coming from each agency go directly to their assigned folder. This way, when companies send you multiple emails about available jobs, you won't see them in your main inbox. Instead, you will be able to browse them whenever you are in the mood by clicking on that agency's folder.

According to Google support, here is how to create a filter for a Gmail account:

1. Open Gmail.
2. In the search box at the top, click the down arrow.
3. Enter your search criteria.
4. At the bottom of the search window, click create filter with this search.
5. Choose what you'd like the filter to do.
6. Click create filter.

Invoicing

When generating invoices it is essential to find a consistent system that is easy to maintain. You will need to decide how soon payment is expected (say, 30 days from the invoice date), and decide on which days you will submit your invoices. It is difficult to keep track of how much money is coming in when you're sending invoices on random days and therefore receiving payment on random days.

As an example, you might choose to submit invoices twice a month; on the 1st and on the 16th. The invoices submitted on the first might include any work you did from the 16th to the end of the month (EOM). The invoices submitted on the 16th might include any work you did from the 1st through the 15th of the current month. For example: you could submit an invoice on January 1st that includes work done from December 16th-EOM, and submit another invoice on January 16th that includes work done from January 1st through the 15th. This way you will only need to focus on invoices and payments twice a month because you are sending all invoices and receiving all payments on the 1st and the 16th (see the following figure).

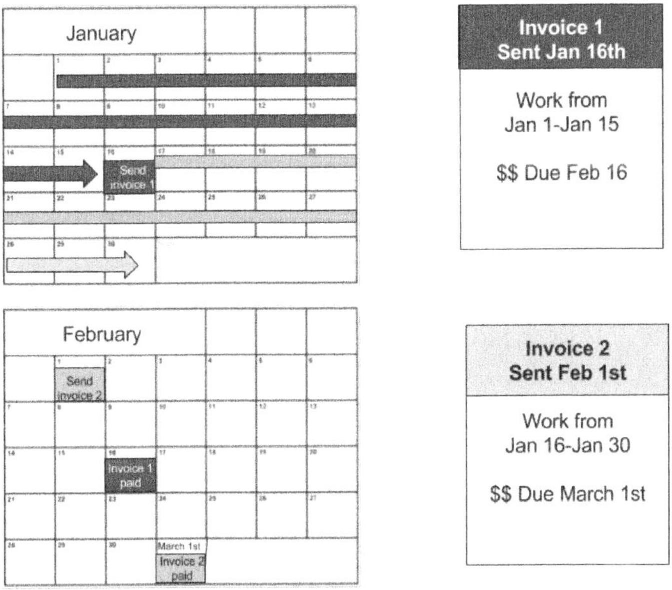

Example of Invoice Scheduling

You will also need to decide on an invoice numbering system. You might choose to label each invoice by the date and the agency name (i.e. 010117AGENCY), or you might start with the year instead of the month for ease of searching through old invoices (i.e. 170101AGENCY). Or you might create a system that relies on a simple numerical sequence (i.e. 00001, 00002, 00003, etc.). However you number your invoices is completely up to you, but once you decide on a system stick to it. If you choose to manually create your invoices there are many templates available online. Below is a sample invoice that has been revised from a free Microsoft Word template.

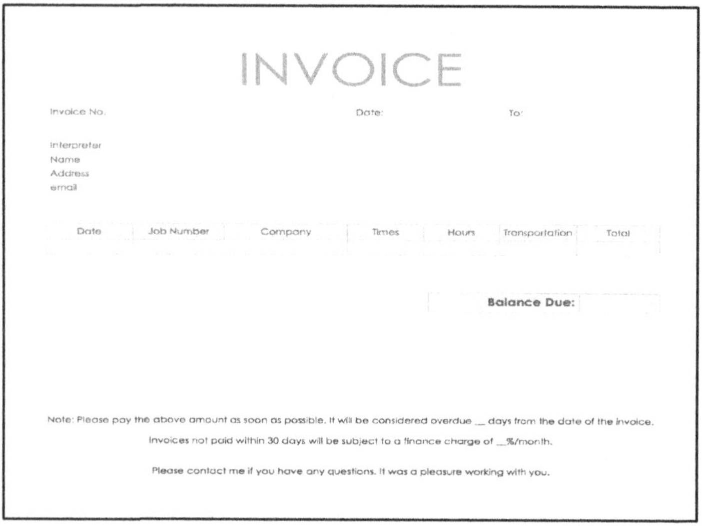

INVOICE

Invoice No. Date: To:

Interpreter
Name
Address
email

Date	Job Number	Company	Times	Hours	Transportation	Total

Balance Due:

Note: Please pay the above amount as soon as possible. It will be considered overdue __ days from the date of the invoice.
Invoices not paid within 30 days will be subject to a finance charge of __%/month.

Please contact me if you have any questions. It was a pleasure working with you.

Sample Invoice Template

It may also be easier to use an online invoicing system such as QuickBooks Online (QBO). You can email invoices directly from QBO to your consumers. You can even set up the option for them to pay you via credit card. When you connect your QuickBooks account to your business bank account (or designated checking account used for business) you will be able to categorize all of your expenses and document when your invoices get paid. This is particularly helpful when you are interpreting for many small agencies and you have to keep track of who owes you payment. QBO's invoicing feature is a great way to track who has, and has not, paid you on time.

Terms and Conditions

Terms and conditions are an agreement that is made when you accept an interpreting assignment. Depending on your particular field they can be anywhere from 1-10 pages.

If you screen with an interpreting agency and accept work through them, often times they have their own set of terms and conditions that you must agree to before you can accept work. These terms and conditions typically include their expectations for professionalism, ethics, billing policies, cancellation policies, etc. Be sure to read through these carefully before signing. Once you have signed, both you and the agency are legally bound to what has been agreed upon. If you decide to pursue direct work on your own, you will need to draft your own set of terms and conditions.

Although it doesn't have to be extensive, it should at least include the following:

Rates

- How much will you charge per hour?
- What is your last-minute rate?
- What constitutes a last-minute request? (Example: *a request made less than 48 hours in advance*)
- Do you have a 2-hour minimum or a flat rate?

- If the assignment is over a certain length, will you require a team interpreter?
- If an assignment goes longer than the agreed upon time frame, how will you bill for the extra time? (Example: *should the interpreter be available to stay overtime, any extra interpreting will be billed by the half hour*)

PAYMENT

- How soon will payment be due? Within how many business days of the invoice date?
- What will happen if they don't pay on time? Will they be charged a late fee?
- Who should you submit your invoice to?
- Where or how will they pay? Direct deposit, check etc.

CANCELLATIONS

- How late can they cancel without being billed in full?

TRANSPORTATION

- Will you include mileage on your invoice?

AGREEMENT

- At the end of the contract you may choose to simply put "By accepting these interpreting services you agree to the above terms and conditions."

Including an agreement statement at the end of the terms and conditions can be helpful if you are finding it difficult to get a formal signature. This simply implies that if they confirm you for the assignment, they are automatically agreeing to your terms. Sample independent contractor terms and conditions can easily be found online. Please consult with a professional to finalize your own terms.

Reputation building and branding

As a freelance interpreter, and a small business owner, it is wise to consider your reputation in the community in which you work. Always aim to maintain a professional, ethical, cooperative, friendly and humble image. Representing yourself and your business well with colleagues, interpreting agencies, and consumers is key to cultivating a good reputation. Customer service is a huge part of an interpreter's career and acquiring an advanced understanding of interpersonal skills should be made a priority. Consider your attire and overall appearance when preparing for assignments and be conscious of how you portray yourself in all work relate settings.

Among the numerous easy steps to make you appear more reputable is 'branding'. Creating a logo for your interpreting business and getting business cards (try Vistaprint or Moo) can work wonders when networking. You may also consider creating a simple website to allow people to book your services more quickly (try Wix or Wordpress).

Be sure to include your logo at the top of your terms and conditions, invoices and any other documents you use in your business. There are lots of websites that can be used to help you create a logo. Freelancer.com, Fiverr.com and Upwork.com are good resources for this, but there are many other sites that specialize in low cost logo design.

Another way to build a reputation is through networking. Research local non-profits related to the interpreting field and volunteer at an event. Volunteering is a great way to give back and meet new colleagues or potential clients at the same time. Always put your best foot forward to maintain an image of respect and reliability within your community.

Conclusion

Interpreters can sometimes make the mistake of being lax in their scheduling, invoicing, billing and professionalism. By staying organized in these areas, you should be able to avoid double booking yourself, getting paid late or overlooking important business-related tasks. The more efficient our business practices are as an interpreter, the more brainpower you will have to do your job and achieve your personal and professional goals.

Chapter Main Points

- Key Concept: Organized business practices save you time in the long run.
- Getting Organized
  - Create a system (recommended book, *Getting Things Done* by David Allen).
- Calendar & Task Apps
  - Paid: Pocket Informant App, Asana.
  - Free: Evernote, any calendar/reminder app.
- Emails
  - Utilize filters to keep your inbox clean.
- Invoicing
  - Choose when to submit invoices and create a clear invoice numbering system.
  - Automatic invoicing can help you keep track of when you get paid.
- Terms and Conditions
  - Include your rate, payment information, agreement statement, cancellation policy and other pertinent information.
- Reputation Building and Branding
  - Maintain a professional image. Network.
  - Create business cards and logo.

TAKE ACTION!

1. What resource(s) will you use to organize your to do items and schedule?

- ☐ Pocket Informant
- ☐ Asana
- ☐ Trello
- ☐ Evernote
- ☐ A calendar app
- ☐ A reminder app
- ☐ A daily, monthly or weekly paper calendar
- ☐ Other: __________

2. When will you organize your email inbox? (Adding folders, filters, etc.)

3. What is your invoicing system?
(Example: *any jobs worked from the 1st to the 15th will be invoiced on the 16th*)

Any jobs worked from _______ to _______ will be invoiced on ________
Any jobs worked from _______ to _______ will be invoiced on ________

How will you number your invoices? (Example: *by date, by agency, by order, etc.)*

4. Answer the following questions to begin creating your terms and conditions.

RATES

- How much will you charge per hour?
- Do you have a 2-hour minimum or a flat rate?
- What is your last minute rate?
- What constitutes a last minute request? (Example: *a request made less than 48 hours in advance*)
- Do you have a 2-hour minimum or a flat rate?
- If the assignment is over a certain length, will you require a team interpreter?
- If an assignment goes longer than the agreed upon time frame, how will you bill for the extra time? (Example: *should the interpreter be available to stay overtime, any extra interpreting will be billed by the half hour*)

PAYMENT

- How soon will payment be due? Within how many business days of the invoice date?
- What will happen if they don't pay on time? Will they be charged a late fee?
- Who should you submit your invoice to?
- Where or how will they pay? Direct deposit, check etc.

Cancellations

- How late can they cancel without being billed in full?

Transportation

- Will you include mileage on your invoice?

Agreement

- At the end of the contract, you may choose to simply put "By accepting these interpreting services, you agree to the above terms and conditions."

5. List five interpreting related non-profits in your area:

6. If you wanted to volunteer at a conference, which committee would you like the most?

- ☐ Chair or Co Chair
- ☐ A/V or tech support
- ☐ Food and beverage
- ☐ Interpreter coordinator
- ☐ Presenter coordinator
- ☐ Program book design
- ☐ Registration
- ☐ Sponsors/exhibitors
- ☐ Support staff/volunteers

7. When I am ready to begin branding, I will...

Use the following company to create my business cards

- ☐ Vistaprint.com
- ☐ Moo.com
- ☐ Gotprint.com
- ☐ Zazzle.com
- ☐ Other: _________

Use the following company to create my website

- ☐ Wix.com
- ☐ Wordpress.com
- ☐ Squarespace.com
- ☐ Other: _________

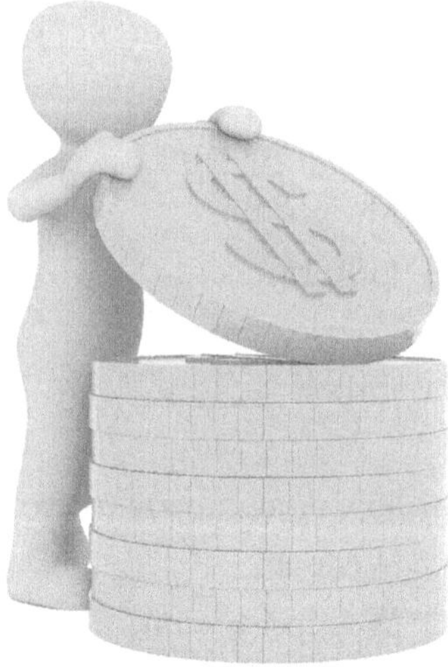

Chapter 6: Retirement Options

We all have personal expenses, and a majority of interpreters graduating from college also have student loan debt to repay, so the idea of saving for retirement may seem daunting. With so much pressure to pay off debt how can one even begin to start saving? Working in your favor is the fact that there are many approaches to retirement saving that freelancers can choose from. In this chapter we will only touch on the following retirement options; Exchange Traded Funds, Traditional IRA, Roth IRA and SEP IRA. To learn more about preparing for retirement please consult a professional financial advisor.

Simple Investing Options

For those who are uninterested in opening a formal retirement account, you can look into apps like *Acorns* (www.Acorns.com). This app can be a good starting point for interpreters just entering the field who don't have much of an income yet. Acorns connects to your bank account. Whenever you make a payment the app rounds the amount up to the nearest dollar and puts that spare change into a stock portfolio of Exchange Traded Funds (stocks or bonds). Another similar option is called *Stash* (www.stashinvest.com). With both of these apps, you can withdraw funds whenever you like. When you do withdraw funds, you will pay taxes on whatever profits you may have incurred. This can be a nice small way to start saving for retirement until you are ready to open a formal retirement account.

Traditional IRA

The Traditional IRA is a long-term investment vehicle. It is an individual retirement account that allows your money to grow, tax-deferred, until you make withdrawals after you reach the retirement age of 59 ½ years or more. This means that any of your IRA contributions can be used as a tax deduction against your income taxes. For example, if you put $6,000 into a traditional IRA account, you will not pay taxes on that money this year. The money is reported as a tax deduction on your personal Federal tax return. You will, however, pay taxes on the amount you contributed, and any interest derived from the contribution amount, at the time of withdrawal (See the following figure). This account can be set up individually without the need of employer involvement.

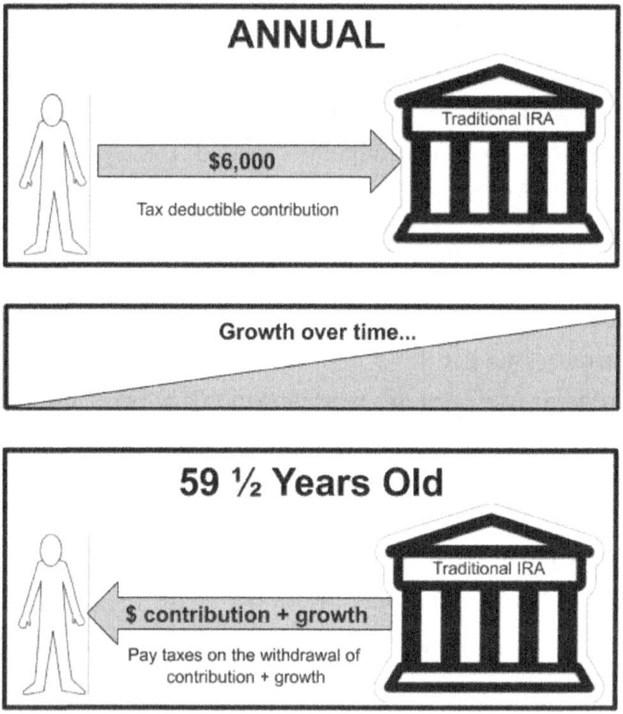

How the Traditional IRA Works

Contribution Limits

The IRS has certain requirements when contributing to your retirement account. As of 2019 there is a $6,000 maximum yearly contribution for a Traditional IRA. The maximum is raised to $7,000 if you're 50+ years old. There are no income limits on those who wish to contribute, and anyone who has earned income can contribute to a Traditional IRA. There are always exceptions to these limitations, however, and we encourage our readers to seek professional advice to fully understand how Traditional IRA accounts work.

Rules of Withdrawal

The IRS states that you cannot withdraw from a Traditional IRA account before you reach the age of 59 ½. If you do withdraw early you will be subject to paying taxes as well as a penalty. You may wait until after 59 ½ years of age to start withdrawing your money but you must begin to withdraw it at least by the age of 70 ½.

Strategy

The IRS states, "a traditional IRA is a way to save for retirement that gives you tax advantages." And, depending on your circumstances, you may be eligible to make fully or partially deductible contributions. Basically, using the Traditional IRA as a means to help lower your yearly tax burden and save for retirement at the same time. Commonly, when a taxpayer retires, they fall into a lower tax bracket than they occupied while working and therefore distributions from the IRA would incur income tax at a lower rate. The strategy here is to predict whether or not you will be in a *lower* tax bracket at retirement age. If you think that you will be in a lower tax bracket at retirement age, you could choose to not pay taxes on your contributions now (at a higher bracket) and instead pay taxes when you withdraw the funds after 59 ½ years of age (at a lower tax bracket).

Roth IRA

The Roth IRA is an individual retirement account that allows a person to use after-tax income to grow their investment tax-free. This means, unlike the Traditional IRA, there is no tax deduction allowed under the Roth IRA. Although, any growth derived from the investment of your contributions will be tax-free. That means you will not have to pay any taxes when you withdraw your money, and the growth accumulated, at retirement age. This account can also be set up individually without the need of employer involvement.

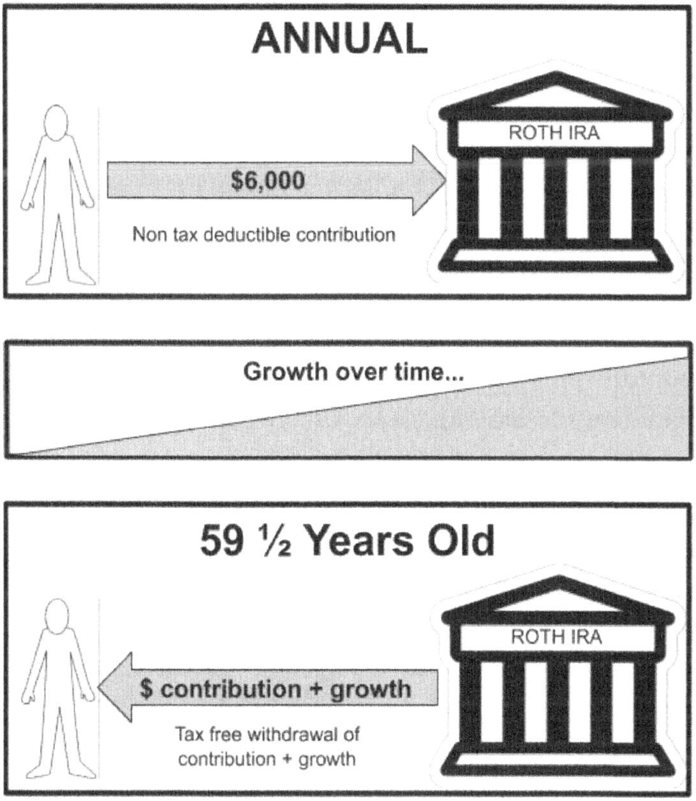

How a Roth IRA works

CONTRIBUTION LIMITS

There is an annual $6,000 maximum contribution limit for a Roth IRA. The maximum is raised to $7,000 if you are age 50 or older. According to the IRS, you can contribute at any age if you, or you and your spouse if filing jointly, have taxable compensation and your modified adjusted gross income is below certain amounts. It is important to recognize that there are always exceptions to these limitations and we encourage our readers to seek professional advice to fully understand how Roth IRA accounts work.

Rules of Withdrawal

With a Roth IRA, you can withdraw any amount of your contributions penalty-free at any time. You cannot withdraw the earnings, or growth, from your contributions penalty-free until after the age of 59 ½. However, there are a few exceptions that allow you to withdraw your earnings before the age of 59 ½. The Roth IRA offers 'qualified distributions' that allow you to make an early withdrawal of both contributions and earnings penalty-free. An example of one such qualified distribution is for a first-time home purchase. If you need to make an early withdrawal please ask a tax professional or financial advisor about all of the qualified distributions criteria you must meet.

Strategy

The strategy here is having the growth from your contributions grow tax-free. Which is the opposite of the Traditional IRA in which you pay taxes on your growth and contributions. Also, it will help if you can predict whether or not you will be in a *higher* tax bracket at retirement age. If you think that you will be in a higher tax bracket at retirement age, you could choose to pay taxes on your contributions now (at a lower tax bracket) and withdraw the funds tax-free after 59 ½ years of age (at a higher tax bracket). Please consult your financial planner to figure out which plan suits you best.

Traditional IRA vs Roth IRA

Features	Traditional IRA	Roth IRA
Who can contribute?	You can contribute if you (or your spouse if filing jointly) have taxable compensation but not after you are age 70½ or older.	You can contribute at any age if you have taxable compensation and your modified adjusted gross income is below certain amounts (see current year limits).
Are my contributions deductible?	You can deduct your contributions if you qualify.	Your contributions aren't deductible.

<table>
<tr><td>How much can I contribute?</td><td colspan="2">The most you can contribute to your Traditional and Roth IRAs is the smaller of: $6,000 (as of 2019), or $7,000 if you're age 50+ by the end of the year; or your taxable compensation.</td></tr>
<tr><td>What is the deadline to make contributions?</td><td colspan="2">Your tax return filing deadline. For example, you can make 2019 IRA contributions until April 15, 2020.</td></tr>
<tr><td>When can I withdraw money?</td><td colspan="2">You can withdraw money anytime. (Penalties may apply)</td></tr>
<tr><td>Do I have to take required minimum distributions?</td><td>You must start taking distributions by April 1 following the year in which you turn age 70½ and by December 31 of later years.</td><td>Not required if you are the original owner.</td></tr>
<tr><td>Are my withdrawals and distributions taxable?</td><td>Any deductible contributions and earnings you withdraw or that are distributed from your traditional IRA are taxable. Also, if you are under age 59 ½ you may have to pay an additional 10% tax for early withdrawals unless you</td><td>None if it's a qualified distribution (or a withdrawal that is a qualified distribution). Otherwise, part of the distribution or withdrawal may be taxable. If you are under age 59 ½, you may also have to pay an additional 10% tax for early withdrawals</td></tr>
</table>

	qualify for an exception.	unless you qualify for an exception.

Traditional IRA vs. Roth IRA

SEP IRA

The SEP IRA provides retirement benefits for both business owners and their employees. This also applies to any self-employed individual including business owners and individuals with freelance income. This type of retirement account takes on some of the characteristics of the Traditional IRA, such as being tax-deductible for the business or employee. This means that the money isn't taxed until it's withdrawn and you cannot withdraw the money prematurely. This account is also nice because of its annual contribution flexibility. The amount of contributions can change depending on how well the business does.

The SEP IRA and a Traditional IRA work pretty much in the same way except for a few distinctions. For the scope of this book there is only one difference that we feel the need to mention: the two plans have different contribution limits. The IRS states that as of 2019, SEP IRA business owners' contribution limit is the lesser of up to 25% of their income, or $56,000. The limit you follow is whichever scenario amounts to the lesser figure. This could be an excellent vehicle for freelancers who want to contribute more to their retirement than is allowed under the Traditional IRA limit of $6,000. Please consult with your financial planner or tax professional to see how much you could contribute to a SEP.

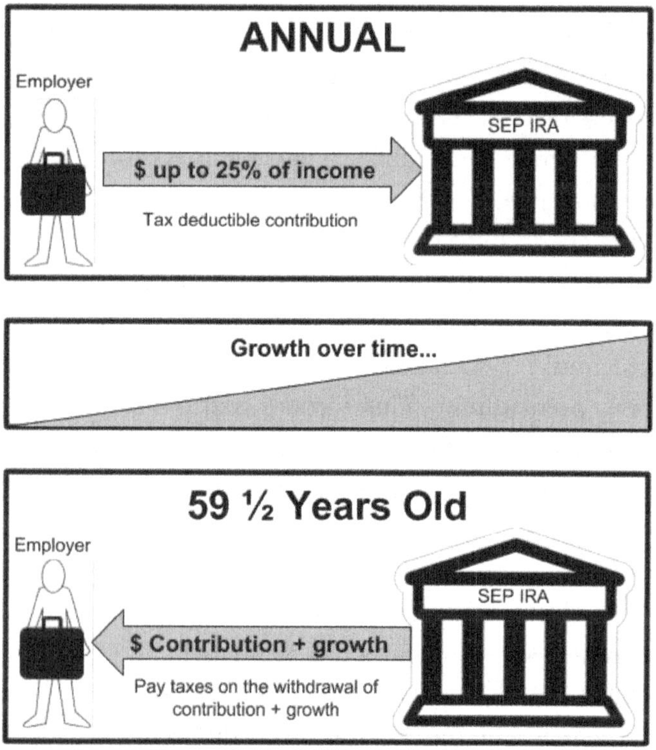

How a SEP IRA works

Conclusion

Best-selling author Chris Hogan explains in his book *Retire Inspired,* that retirement is a financial number; not an age.

In theory, individuals can "retire" as soon as their retirement account balances support their living expenses. As we mentioned earlier, often interpreters shy away from becoming freelance because they don't want to lose the retirement plan that comes with their salaried position. The main take away from this chapter is that freelancers have several different kinds of retirement accounts you can implement especially if you are a business owner or self-employed. Even a combination of different IRA accounts can be a very viable strategy (for example, a SEP IRA and a Roth IRA). Deciding how much you want to contribute each year, and whether you want to pay tax now or later, will help you in figuring out which plan works best for you. When you are ready to open a retirement account please contact a professional financial advisor for guidance and help getting your accounts set up. You can also research online platforms like www.Betterment.com that offer similar retirement accounts.

CHAPTER MAIN POINTS

- Key Concept: Freelancers can get their own retirement account(s).
- Simple Investing
    - Apps like 'Acorns' or 'Stash' are a good fit for those with limited income.

Individual Retirement Accounts		
	Non-Deductible Contribution & Tax Free Withdrawal	Deductible Contribution & Pay taxes on the Withdrawal
Traditional IRA		✓
Roth IRA	✓	
SEP IRA		✓

TAKE ACTION!

1. Of the retirement options listed in this chapter, which one(s) are you most interested in?

- ☐ Simple investing (apps like Acorns or Stash)
- ☐ Traditional IRA
- ☐ SEP IRA (small business owners/employers)
- ☐ ROTH IRA
- ☐ Other: ___________

Reminder:

When you are ready to open a retirement account, please contact a financial advisor for guidance and help getting your accounts set up. You can also research online platforms, like www.Betterment.com, that offer similar support.

CHAPTER 7: INSURANCE

Another reason many people are hesitant to be self-employed is the task of handling your own insurances, particularly health, dental and vision. Depending on where you live there will be different resources and protocols for receiving self-employed insurance. A quick Google search will reveal how simple it can be to find your state's local self-employed or small business owner insurance options.

Health, Dental and Vision

Once you locate your state's healthcare website you will most likely be asked a series of questions and will then be presented with a variety of health care plans that fit your needs. Your state's system may ask you to choose a health insurance plan and then offer you options to add dental and vision later. For those who are new to health care in the United States, individuals pay monthly health insurance fees/premiums to ensure that they will be covered when they need to go to the doctor, clinic or hospital. When choosing your health insurance plan take notice of whether it's an HMO, PPO or other type of plan. There are advantages and disadvantages to both.

HMO vs. PPO Health Insurance Plans		
	PPO	**HMO**
Access to a network of doctors, hospitals and other healthcare providers	✓	✓
Ability to see the doctor you want without a primary care physician (PCP) to authorize treatment	✓	
Referral from a primary care physician (PCP) not needed to see a specialist	✓	
Low or no deductible and generally lower premiums		✓

HMOs vs PPOs

Sole proprietors, single member LLCs and LLC S Corps are allowed to deduct their health insurance premiums on their federal tax return. Keep in mind that the reporting requirements are stricter for S Corps to take this deduction. Please consult a tax professional for more details on how to do this.

Disability Insurance & Workers Compensation

As interpreters, our body is our career. Therefore, if you were to get injured or ill in a way that prevented you from interpreting, your business would severely suffer. Disability insurance covers two situations, (1) being disabled from an accident or an illness, and (2) loss of bodily function such as the loss of a limb or an organ. In the event of a disabling injury or illness, disability insurance would pay a portion of your regular earnings because you cannot perform your primary business duties. This is distinctly different from workers compensation, which makes payments to you for a temporary injury or acquired occupational disease, contracted at your place of work. There are many different types of disability insurance policies including some that don't start to distribute payments until after 90 days. So depending on your plan, it may be important to have three months' worth of income saved to give you a cushion should this occur. Although the process of getting insurance can be a bit lengthy (sometimes including a health exam), in the long run it can be a very comforting feeling to have disability insurance just in case.

Conclusion

Insurance is available to single member small business owners like freelance interpreters and signing up for these policies isn't as daunting as some would assume. Some interpreters may opt to buy only health, dental and vision insurance in the beginning and add liability, workers compensation and disability later. Others may choose to never get liability, workers compensation or disability insurance. Some may get all three right away. Everyone's situation is unique and we encourage each reader to do whatever gives them the most peace of mind and protection. We also encourage readers to talk to a professional about different insurance and workers compensation plans available to them.

Chapter Main Points

- Key Concept: Interpreters can get insurance as self-employed business owners.
- Health, Dental & Vision
    - Can be obtained through your state's healthcare exchange website.
- Liability
    - Offers protection if you get sued for accidentally misinterpreting information or causing property damage on a job.
- Disability
    - Offers coverage if the injury or illness results in becoming a disability and you are unable to interpret.
- Workers Compensation
    - Offers coverage if you injure yourself on the job and need compensation temporarily.

TAKE ACTION!

1. What type of Health insurance plan do you want?

- ☐ PPO
- ☐ HMO

2. Let's start researching!

1. Google search "Health insurance in __________(your state)"

2. What options are there for small business owners or sole proprietors?

3. When is open season? This is the window of time when you can purchase your health insurance for the following year.

4. How does your state handle Dental and Vision? Is it an "add on" after you sign up for health insurance?

3. Do you plan on getting Liability Insurance?

- ☐ Yes
- ☐ No
- ☐ Not sure yet

If you answered yes, or not sure, go ahead and Google search "liability insurance for interpreters." Write down at least 3 companies that you will contact for a quote.

4. Do you plan on getting Disability Insurance?

- ☐ Yes
- ☐ No
- ☐ Not sure yet

If you answered yes, or not sure, go ahead and Google search "disability insurance for interpreters." Write down at least 3 companies that you will contact for a quote.

CHAPTER 8: SELF-CARE

Much like a professional dancer or athlete, our most important business asset is our body. An asset, from a business perspective, is something valuable a business owns that generates income. An interpreter's career revolves around our physical bodies. An interpreter's voice, hearing, hands (for sign language interpreters), arms, shoulders, back, legs and mind are the assets of your business. The act of interpreting can be taxing physically, mentally and often times emotionally. This is why it is important to take care of ourselves, remain balanced and, in turn, take care of the service we provide.

Physical Self Care

Take time to consider your physical state. Are your muscles tight? Do you have any aches and pains? Do you get headaches often? These issues, as minor as they may seem in the present moment, can add up and eventually put your career at risk. As we mentioned above, interpreters can benefit from viewing their bodies in the same way a professional athlete does. Consider whether you're taking enough breaks, getting frequent massages, stretching, getting enough sleep, drinking plenty of water, eating healthy, exercising regularly, breathing deeply. If your work requires that you stand for long periods of time, pay attention to the quality of your shoes. If your work requires that you sit for long periods of time, try to find opportunities to stand up and walk around, stretch or be active. As an interpreter, bodily pain or discomfort can be extremely distracting to your work. Your body is your instrument. Take care of it.

Emotional Self Care

As an interpreter, other people's thoughts, opinions and feelings are channeled through you every day. If you happen to be interpreting a heated conversation, or an emotional moment, it is common to experience vicarious trauma or burnout. If you interpret something stressful it's wise to seek out trusted colleagues to debrief with. By attempting to simply brush off an emotionally charged interpreting assignment, you may find it becomes a trigger and begins to impact your work in other settings.

Notice any anxiety you may feel before or after your assignments as well. If there are individuals or settings that cause consistent stress perhaps consider not working there as frequently. There is a time to push oneself and try new environments, and there's a time to accept that if something is causing anxiety repeatedly it may not be a good fit. Find healthy tools to help in these moments of stress or anxiety; therapy, essential oils, positive conversations with yourself or others, meditation, journaling, breathing, music, coloring or whatever helps you unwind.

As a reminder, waking up early and arriving at your assignments with plenty of time to spare can work wonders for anxiety. The calmer and more collected an interpreter feels, the better they will be on the job. Find ways to stay centered going into each assignment.

Take care of your emotional state at the end of each day. Reconnect with your own identity and your own thoughts. Find a way to express your uniqueness. When we spend our entire career *being* other people, we can easily begin to lose a sense of self or become burnt out. Find outlets to stay true to yourself, do things that bring you joy and, as we mentioned above, take breaks as needed. Breaks don't have to be limited to short rests throughout the workday, they can also include vacations or weekend getaways.

Mental Self Care

Personal growth and professional development is an important part of a balanced life. If we're not growing as individuals, we can start to feel stuck, or frustrated, in our careers. We are meant to expand our horizons as we get older, so it's important to incorporate that into your interpreting careers and lives.

Some examples of growth can include reading books or watching documentaries on topics that interest you. Attending conferences, workshops, or seminars can all be very stimulating. Consider what hobbies outside of interpreting you'd like to pursue. You can even set goals for yourself to monitor your growth outside your day-to-day career.

There are many approaches to personal goal setting. One, inspired by Anthony Robbins, is creating a life wheel. This is a great exercise to assess how much balance you have in your current life by looking at the following categories: career, social life, personal growth, health, family, relationships, finance and attitude.

Here's a breakdown of how you can use the wheel:

1. Write a note on what a "10" would look like to you in each of the categories on the following chart.

2. Rate where you are currently in each category on a scale from 1-10.

3. If you notice you're not at a 10. Set up a SMART goal (Specific, Measurable, Achievable, Realistic, and Timely) to help you reach a 10.

4. Create an actionable plan for how you will get to a 10 in each category.

5. Do this exercise monthly, quarterly or annually to monitor your progress.

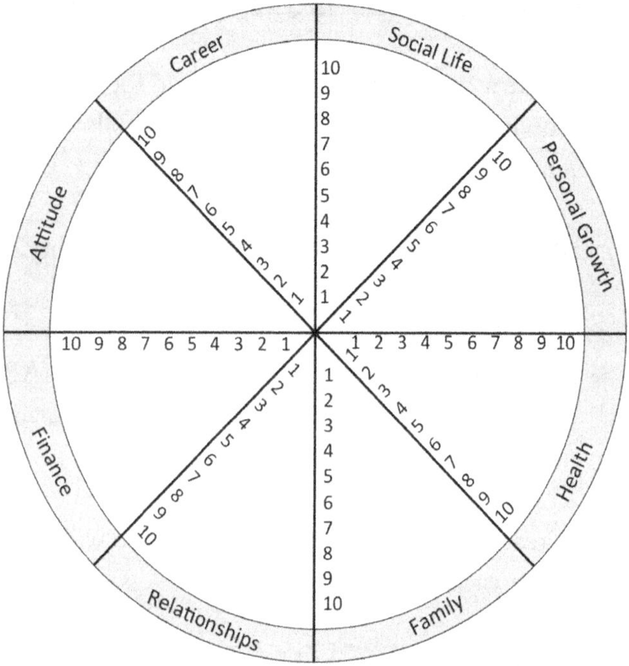

Life Wheel

Conclusion

At the end of the day, our health is a guiding factor in how our daily experiences turn out. By prioritizing self-care, interpreters will not only lengthen their careers but they may also have more energy to grow professionally. By prioritizing and investing in your most important asset (your body), you are also investing in your business, your happiness, your health, and your overall quality of life.

Chapter Main Points

- Key Concept: Prioritizing self-care can lead to business success and longevity.
- Physical Self Care
    - Your career is dependent on your physical ability to interpret.
    - Drink water, get enough sleep, eat healthy, exercise, breathe deeply, take breaks etc.
- Emotional Self Care
    - Be aware of burnout and vicarious trauma.
    - Take care of your emotional state everyday.
- Mental Self Care
    - Find ways to express yourself, learn and grow.
    - Complete a Life Wheel to create goals and stick to them.

TAKE ACTION!

1. This list contains examples of physical stress relieving activities. Choose at least one to begin implementing now.

- □ Exercise.
- □ Light a candle.
- □ Get a hot water bottle or a heating pad. When you feel stressed put it on your stomach or lower back.
- □ Listen to classical music.
- □ Stretch in the morning.
- □ Drink enough water during the day (aim for ½ of your body weight in ounces).
- □ Get enough sleep. Also try to be consistent with your wake-up time.
- □ Wake up 15 minutes earlier than you normally would. Do not start your day in a rushed or reactive mode.
- □ Prepare for the next day the night before.
- □ Say "no" to things. Give yourself enough breaks.
- □ Once a day, sit quietly and breathe deeply for 5 minutes.
- □ Journal daily for at least 5 minutes.

2. Now let's plan ahead and prepare how you will handle burnout, or a break down.

MY BREAKDOWN PLAN:

If I am having a breakdown, or feel burnt out, I will do the following:

Example: I will get a drink of water, find a place to be alone, listen to classical music and breathe deeply for 5 minutes. Then I will journal about what is upsetting me.

MY "AT WORK" BREAKDOWN PLAN:

If I feel a breakdown coming, or if I feel burnt out while I'm in a work setting, I will do the following:

Example: I will excuse myself to the restroom, do a few simple stretches, and breathe deeply.

3. Look at the Life Wheel and answer the following questions:

1. Write out what a "10" would look like to you in the following categories.
2. Rate yourself in each category from 1-10 on where you are currently.
3. If you notice you're not at a 10, set up a SMART (Specific, Measurable, Achievable, Realistic, and Timely) to help you reach a 10.
4. Create an actionable plan for how you will get to a 10 in each category.
5. Do this exercise monthly, quarterly or annually to monitor your progress.

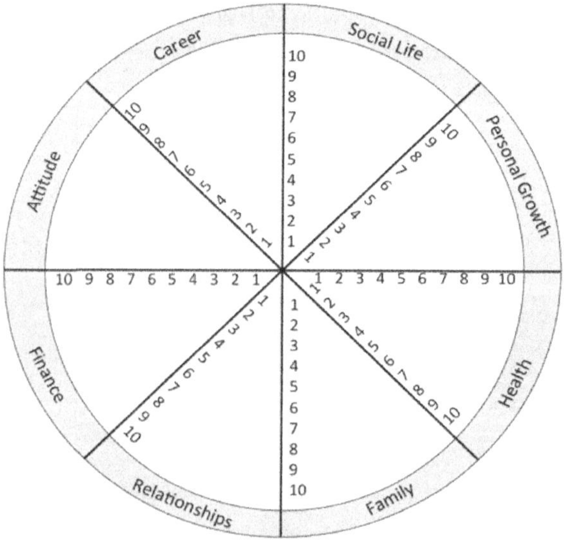

CHAPTER 9: CONCLUSION

When a freelance interpreter enters the field they may, or may not, view themselves as a small business owner. By approaching freelancing as a small business we can save money and lessen our tax burden by learning from other small business models. When interpreters re-frame how they view themselves and their work, many new opportunities for growth can unfold.

A common complaint amongst freelancers is that they pay too much in taxes. We can learn a lot by observing how businesses approach tax classification, entity structuring, tax deductions, bookkeeping, organization, retirement, insurance and even how they care for their employees. By observing other businesses we can learn a great deal about how we, as interpreters, can use similar approaches to thrive in our profession.

We hope the information in this book motivates each reader to continue learning and researching on their own in order to discover their unique preferences in building their business as an interpreter. It's always a good idea to build rapport with a good tax professional, financial planner, and/or attorney to guide you on this journey towards successful small business ownership. Whether you are a new freelancer entering the interpreting field, a seasoned freelancer looking for a brush up, or anything in between, we hope you will continue to use this book throughout your career as a quick reference guide to interpreting business practices.

Compiled Chapter Main Points

TAXES

- Key Concept: Understanding how freelancers and W-2 employees are taxed.

Types of Tax	How Much we Pay
Social Security & Medicare tax *Known as "FICA" for employees, or "Self-employment Tax" for freelancers*	15.3% (Social Security: 12.4%, Medicare: 2.9%)
Federal Income Tax	Percent based on brackets
State & Local Income Tax	Percent varies by state

	Employee	Independent Contractor
Form you fill out	W-4	W-9
Form you receive	W-2	1099
How taxes are paid	The employer pays on your behalf	You pay estimated taxes quarterly

Business Structures

- Key Concept: Understand different entity structures.

Entity	Advantages	Disadvantages
Sole Proprietor	Cheapest and easiest to setup.	No asset protection. Taxed on all earnings (FICA + income tax).
LLC Tax status: Sole Proprietor	Asset protection.	Must comply with regulations (meetings, records, etc.). Taxed on all earnings (FICA + income tax).
LLC Tax election: S Corp	Asset protection. Taxed fully on W-2 employee salary (FICA + Income Tax). Taxed less on shareholder's distribution (Income Tax only).	Must comply with regulations (meetings, records, etc.). More complicated to set up, FUTA tax and an extra filing fee.

DEDUCTIONS

- Key Concept: Save money by using business expense deductions.
- Business deductions are ONLY for business expenses. If an item is used for business 50% of the time, only deduct 50% of its cost or running expense.

Start-up Cost Deductions: $10,000		
Start-up Cost	**Organizational Cost**	**Capital Expense**
$5,000 allowed.	$5,000 allowed. Not applicable for Sole Proprietors.	Expensive assets depreciated over life span of the item.

Car Deductions	
Actual Car Expense Method	**Standard Mileage Method**
CAN deduct gas, oil change, lease, insurance, etc. CANNOT deduct mileage.	CAN deduct mileage. CANNOT deduct expenses from Actual Car Expense Method.

Traveling		
With Home Office	**Without Home Office**	**Working out of State**
CAN deduct round trip to and from home.	CAN deduct commute in-between jobs. CANNOT deduct commute to and from home.	CAN deduct travel expenses.

Home Office Deduction	
Regular Method	**Simplified Method**
Based on the percent of house used for the office.	Multiply $5 by the square footage of your office.

Meals
50% of the cost is deductible if with colleagues or clients for business matters locally. For traveling out of town, eating alone is acceptable.

Bookkeeping

- Key Concept: Stay organized and separate business and personal finances.
- Banking
    - Separate your business and personal finances.

Accounting 101	
Cash Accounting	**Accrual Accounting**
Document money as you receive/spend it.	Document money following the invoice/billing date.

- Record Keeping
    - Keep track of your expenses with detail in the event an audit happens.
- Bookkeeping Software
    - A Chart of Accounts keeps your expenses organized for tax deductions.
    - Profit and loss reports can provide you with 'the big picture' of how you are doing financially.
    - Keep track of your business expenses in case the IRS audits you.

Use a Budget to Guide your Schedule (example)	
Steps	**What to do**
1	Monthly expenses (including extra to cover taxes): $3,250.
2	Divide this number by your freelance rate: $3250/ $45 = 72 hours per month.
3	Divide this number by 4: 72/4 = you need to work at least 18 hours per week to cover your spending habits.

- Creating a System: How to Stay within Budget
    - Manual: Spreadsheets
    - Paid Systems:
    - YouNeedABudget.com
    - Free Systems:
        - Mint.com
        - DaveRamsey.com/Everydollar
        - Banking apps

Business Practices

- Key Concept: Organized business practices save you time in the long run.
- Getting Organized
  - Create a system (recommended book, *Getting Things Done* by David Allen).
- Calendar & Task Apps
  - Paid: Pocket Informant App, Asana.
  - Free: Evernote, any calendar/reminder app.
- Emails
  - Utilize filters to keep your inbox clean.
- Invoicing
  - Choose when to submit invoices and create a clear invoice numbering system.
  - Automatic invoicing can help you keep track of when you get paid.
- Terms and Conditions
  - Include your rate, payment information, agreement statement, cancellation policy and other pertinent information.
- Reputation Building and Branding
  - Maintain a professional image. Network.
  - Create business cards and logo.

Retirement Options

- Key Concept: Freelancers can get their own retirement account(s).
- Simple Investing
    - Apps like 'Acorns' or 'Stash' are a good fit for those with limited income.

Individual Retirement Accounts		
	Non Deductible Contribution & Tax Free Withdrawal	Deductible Contribution & Pay taxes on the Withdrawal
Traditional IRA		✓
Roth IRA	✓	
SEP IRA		✓

INSURANCE

- Key Concept: Interpreters can get insurance as self-employed business owners.
- Health, Dental & Vision
    - Can be obtained through your state's healthcare exchange website.
- Liability
    - Offers protection if you get sued for accidentally misinterpreting information or causing property damage on a job.
- Disability
    - Offers coverage if the injury or illness results in becoming a disability and you are unable to interpret.
- Workers Compensation
    - Offers coverage if you injure yourself on the job and need compensation temporarily.

Self Care

- Key Concept: Prioritizing self-care can lead to business success and longevity.
- Physical Self Care
    - Your career is dependent on your physical ability to interpret.
    - Drink water, get enough sleep, eat healthy, exercise, breathe deeply, take breaks etc.
- Emotional Self Care
    - Be aware of burnout and vicarious trauma.
    - Take care of your emotional state everyday.
- Mental Self Care
    - Find ways to express yourself, learn and grow.
    - Complete a Life Wheel to create goals and stick to them.

About the Authors

Rosemary Johnson, MA, NIC

Professional Tax Preparer & Speaker

Originally from Illinois, Rosemary has been an American Sign Language interpreter and small business owner since 2011. Her educational background consists of a Bachelor's degree in American Sign Language (ASL) – English Interpretation, and a Master's degree in Deaf Studies: Culture; both of which she obtained from Gallaudet University. Her masters thesis explored the use of ASL Mobile Access Technology in museums and received the Excellence in Research and Writing Award, which is given to only one student every year. Rosemary currently holds the National Interpreting Certification (NIC) from the Registry of Interpreters for the Deaf (RID), which she earned in 2012. Her professional interpreting experience includes, but is not limited to: government, business, post-secondary education, DeafBlind, performing arts and platform. She has served four years on the Executive Board for the Potomac Chapter of the Registry of Interpreters for the Deaf (PCRID). Rosemary is also a highly sought-after presenter, professional tax preparer, a co-owner of Quick Guide Tax, and enjoys working with interpreters to apply concepts from this book into their business practices.

Brent Bocian, MAI, NIC, SC:L

QuickBooks ProAdvisor & Ramsey Solutions Financial Coach

Mr. Bocian began his business endeavors while being a board member of MB Custom Wood Finishing, LLC, where he oversaw business operations for more than 10 years. Upon leaving MB Custom he established a business of his own by co-founding Single Swing, LLC, an online golf retail company. He is also a co-owner of Quick Guide Tax where he offers his services as a QuickBooks ProAdvisor and Ramsey Solutions Financial Coach. In addition to his business and LLC operations experience, Mr. Bocian currently holds the National Interpreting Certification (NIC) from the Registry of Interpreters for the Deaf (RID), which he earned in 2008. His professional interpreting experience includes, but is not limited to: government, VRS/VRI, business, post-secondary education, medical, Deaf-Blind, sports, and legal settings. Mr. Bocian was awarded the Specialized Certificate: Legal, SC:L in 2015. He mentored and apprenticed under the supervision of seasoned legal interpreters Carla Mathers and Patty Moers-Patterson. Mr. Bocian's educational background consists of a Bachelor's degree in ASL-English Interpreting from the National Technical Institute for the Deaf (NTID) at the Rochester Institute of Technology (RIT). Additionally, he received his Master's degree in Interpretation from Gallaudet University where he conducted research regarding VRS interpreting through the lens of the Demand Control Schema.

REFERENCES

Accounting Equation | Explanation | Accounting Coach. (n.d.). Retrieved from https://www.accountingcoach.com/accounting-equation/explanation, August 4, 2017

Allen, D., Getting Things Done: The Art of Stress-Free Productivity, Penguin Books, New York, NY, 2015

Botkin, S., CPA, ESQ. Lower Your Taxes - BIG TIME! 2017-2018 Edition: Wealth Building, Tax Reduction Secrets from an IRS Insider (7th ed.), McGraw-Hill Education, New York, NY, 2017

Bower, K. (2015).Stress and Burnout in Video Relay Service (VRS) Interpreting.*Journal of Interpretation, 24*(1), 1-16. Retrieved August 4, 2017, from http://digitalcommons.unf.edu/cgi/viewcontent.cgi?article=1047&context=joi

Carla Mathers http://www.streetleverage.com/2012/01/how-practicing-sign-language-interpreters-protect-against-legal-liability/

Compare Best Credit Card Offers | Car Insurance | CD Rates | Savings. (n.d.). Retrieved August 4, 2017, from https://www.nerdwallet.com/

Cooper, C. (n.d.). How to Open an LLC Bank Account. Retrieved August 4, 2017, from http://info.legalzoom.com/open-llc-bank-account-3455.html

Cummings, E. (2015, August 10). Understanding the U.S. Health Care System. InterExchange. Retrieved August 21, 2017, from https://www.interexchange.org/articles/abroad/2015/08/10/understanding-us-healthcare-system/

Estimate your taxes. (n.d.). Retrieved October 14, 2017, from http://www.irscalculators.com/tax-brackets-calculator

Ferriss, T., The 4-Hour Workweek: Escape 9-5, Live Anywhere, and Join the New Rich, Harmony, New York, N, 2009

Form an LLC or Corporation, New Business & Incorporate Online. (n.d.). Retrieved August 4, 2017, from https://www.bizfilings.com/

Get organized. Work smarter. Remember everything. (n.d.). Retrieved August 4, 2017, from https://evernote.com/

Getting Things Done Model [Digital image]. (n.d.). Retrieved August 4 ,2017, from http://paulminors.com/wp-content/uploads/2015/04/Getting-Things-Done-Model.png

HMO vs. PPO Insurance Plans. (n.d.). Retrieved August 4, 2017, from https://www.medmutual.com/For-Individuals-and-Families/Health-Insurance-Education/Compare-Health-Insurance-Plans/HMO-vs-PPO-Insurance

Hogan, C. (2016). *Retire Inspired: It's not an Age, it's a Financial Number.* Brentwood, TN: Lampo Licensing, LLC

Inglese, C. J. (2017). *Tax strategies for the one-person business.* CreateSpace Independent Publishing Platform.

Insureon. (2015, April 23). Professional liability vs. errors and omissions insurance. Retrieved May 13, 2019, from https://www.insureon.com/blog/post/2015/04/23/professional-liability-vs-errors-omissions-insurance-whats-the-difference.aspx

Internal Revenue Service. (n.d.). Retrieved August 21, 2017, from https://www.irs.gov/

Internal Revenue Service (2018). *Revenue Procedure 2018-57.* Retrieved May 2nd, 2019, from https://www.irs.gov/pub/irs-drop-rp-18-57.pdf

J.K. Lassers Your Income Tax 2019. (2019). Hoboken, NJ: John Wiley & Sons.

Kohler, M. J. (2015). The tax and legal playbook: game-changing solutions to your small business questions. Irvine, CA: Entrepreneur Press.

Manson, M., The Subtle Art of Not Giving a F*ck: A Counterintuitive Approach to Living a Good Life, HarperCollins Publishers, New York, NY, 2016

McQuown, J. H. Inc. *Yourself: How to Profit By Setting Up Your Own Corporation*(9th ed.), Broadway, Portland, OR, 2000

Mueller, R. R. (2018). *America's New 2018 Tax Cuts and Jobs Act.* San Diego, CA: Home Business Tax Savings.

Pocket Informant is the Best Calendar for iOS, mac, and Android. (n.d.). Retrieved August 4, 2017, from https://www.pocketinformant.com/

Publication 463 (2016), Travel, Entertainment, Gift, and Car Expenses. (n.d.). Retrieved August 21, 2017, from https://www.irs.gov/publications/p463/ch05.html

Publication 463 (2016), Travel, Entertainment, Gift, and Car Expenses. (n.d.). Retrieved August 21, 2017, from https://www.irs.gov/publications/p463/ch02.html#en_US_2016_publink100033878

Publication 463 (2016), Travel, Entertainment, Gift, and Car Expenses. (n.d.). Retrieved August 21, 2017, from https://www.irs.gov/publications/p463/ch01.html

Pursue your passion. We'll handle your books. (n.d.). Retrieved August 4, 2017, from http://quickbooks.intuit.com/

Rethink What Your Money Can Do. (n.d.). Retrieved August 4, 2017, from https://www.betterment.com/

Retirement Plans. (n.d.). Retrieved August 4, 2017, from https://www.irs.gov/retirement-plans

Richards, T. J. (2008). Establishing a freelance interpretation business: professional guidance for sign language interpreters. Hillsboro, OR: Butte Publications

Robbins, T., *Unshakeable: Your Financial Freedom Playbook*, Simon & Schuster, New York, NY, 2017

Shareholder's Instructions for Schedule K-1 (2017). Retrieved January 7, 2018, from https://www.irs.gov/instructions/i1120ssk#idm140651237078672

Simplified Option for Home Office Deduction. (2016, October 28). Retrieved August 21, 2017, from https://www.irs.gov/businesses/small-businesses-self-employed/simplified-option-for-home-office-deduction

Small Business Administration. (n.d.). Retrieved August 21, 2017, from https://www.sba.gov/

Small Business/Self-Employed Topics. (n.d.). Retrieved August 4, 2017, from https://www.irs.gov/businesses/small-businesses-self-employed/simplified-option-for-home-office-deduction

Smith, C. (n.d.). Cash vs. Accrual Accounting: What's Best for Your Small Business? Retrieved August 4, 2017, from http://quickbooks.intuit.com/r/bookkeeping/cash-vs-accrual-accounting-whats-best-small-business/

Soto, S. (2010). How to start your own language translation & interpreter business: the complete "How-To" guide for language interpreters, translators and professionals starting their own language translation business. Bloomington, IN: AuthorHouse.

Sutton, G., ESQ., &Detweiler, G., *Finance Your Own Business: Get on the Financing Fast Track*, Success DNA, Inc., Minden, NV, 2016

Sutton, G., ESQ., Run Your Own Corporation: How to Legally Operate and Properly Maintain Your Company Into the Future (2nd ed., Rich Dad Advisors), RDA Press, LLC, Scottsdale, AZ, 2012

Sutton, G. (2016). Start your own corporation: why the rich own their own companies and everyone else works for them. Scottsdale, AZ: RDA Press, LLC.

Tax Brackets 2017: How They Work, Examples, & Myths. (2017, October 09). Retrieved October 14, 2017, from https://blog.taxact.com/how-tax-brackets-work/?utm_source=TaxACT&utm_medium=Tax-Bracket-Calculator&utm_campaign=Learn-More

Tax Cut and Jobs Act, Public Law No: 115-97 (2017). Retrieved from https://www.congress.gov/bill/115th-congress/house-bill/1/text

Tony Robbins RPM: Categories of Improvement. (n.d.). Retrieved August 4, 2014, from http://www.time-management-techniques.com/tony-robbins-rpm.html

Tracy, J. A. (1997). *Accounting for dummies.* Wiley & Sons, Incorporated, John.

Traditional and Roth IRAs. (2017, January 30). Retrieved August 21, 2017, from https://www.irs.gov/retirement-plans/traditional-and-roth-iras

Use Asana to track your team's work & manage projects · Asana. (n.d.). Retrieved August 4, 2017, from https://asana.com/

Vranich, B., Dr., Breathe: The Simple, Revolutionary 14-Day Program to Improve Your Mental and Physical Health, New York, NY: St. Martin's Press, 2016

Weil, A., M.D., 8 Weeks to Optimum Health: A Proven Program for Taking Full Advantage of Your Body's Natural Healing Power, Random House Publishing Group, New York, NY, 2007

Wheelwright, T., CPA. *Tax-Free Wealth: How to Build Massive Wealth by Permanently Lowering Your Taxes* (Rich Dad Advisors), RDA Press, LLC., Scottsdale, AZ, 2012

Willink, J., &Babin, L. *Extreme Ownership: How U.S. Navy SEALs Lead and Win*, St. Martin's Press, New York, NY, 2015

YNAB. Personal Budgeting Software for Windows, Mac, iOS and Android. (n.d.). Retrieved August 4, 2017, from https://www.youneedabudget.com/

Zafar, N., *Finance Essentials for Entrepreneurs*, Five Mountain Press, Silicon Valley, CA, 2010

Made in the USA
Middletown, DE
21 January 2021

32127701R00096